PUBLIC MANAGEMENT DEVELOPMENTS

UPDATE 1991

ORGANISATION FOR ECONOMIC CO-OPERATION AND DEVELOPMENT

Pursuant to Article 1 of the Convention signed in Paris on 14th December 1960, and which came into force on 30th September 1961, the Organisation for Economic Co-operation and Development (OECD) shall promote policies designed:

— to achieve the highest sustainable economic growth and employment and a rising standard of living in Member countries, while maintaining financial stability, and thus to contribute to the development of the world economy;

— to contribute to sound economic expansion in Member as well as non-member countries in the process of economic development; and

— to contribute to the expansion of world trade on a multilateral, non-discriminatory basis in accordance with international obligations.

The original Member countries of the OECD are Austria, Belgium, Canada, Denmark, France, Germany, Greece, Iceland, Ireland, Italy, Luxembourg, the Netherlands, Norway, Portugal, Spain, Sweden, Switzerland, Turkey, the United Kingdom and the United States. The following countries became Members subsequently through accession at the dates indicated hereafter: Japan (28th April 1964), Finland (28th January 1969), Australia (7th June 1971) and New Zealand (29th May 1973). The Commission of the European Communities takes part in the work of the OECD (Article 13 of the OECD Convention). Yugoslavia takes part in some of the work of the OECD (agreement of 28th October 1961).

Publié en français sous le titre :

ÉVOLUTIONS DANS LA GESTION PUBLIQUE
MISE À JOUR 1991

This report is an update of *Public Management Developments: Survey — 1990* (OECD, Paris, 1990) which described developments in public sector management in Member countries up to the end of 1989. It reflects the situation as reported by Member countries at the end of 1990.

The report was compiled by David Rushforth of the OECD Secretariat in close collaboration with a network of national correspondents designated by Member countries for this purpose (see Annex I). The Public Management Committee reviewed the report on 8 April 1991 and recommended that it be made available to the public. It is published on the responsibility of the Secretary-General.

ALSO AVAILABLE

Administration as Service: The Public as Client (1987)
(42 87 01 1) ISBN 92-64-12946-4   FF90   £9.00   US$18.00   DM40
Public Management Developments. Survey 1990 (1990)
(42 90 03 1) ISBN 92-64-13437-9   FF130   £16.00   US$28.00   DM50
Public Management Studies. Flexible Personnel Management in the Public Service (1990)
(42 90 01 1) ISBN 92-64-13353-4   FF90   £11.00   US$19.00   DM35
The Control and Management of Government Expenditure (1987)
(42 87 02 1) ISBN 92-64-12995-2   FF130   £13.00   US$27.00   DM56

Cut along dotted line
-- --

ORDER FORM

Please enter my order for:

Qty.	Title	Price
....	....	....
....	....	....
....	....	....
....	....	....
		_____
	Total :	....

- Payment is enclosed ☐
- Charge my VISA card ☐   Number of card ....
  (Note: You will be charged the French franc price.)
  Expiration of card .... *Signature* ....
- *Send invoice. A purchase order is attached* ☐

Send publications to *(please print):*

Name ....

Address ....

....

....

Send this Order Form to OECD Publications Service, 2, rue André-Pascal, 75775 PARIS CEDEX 16, France, or to OECD Publications and Information Centre or Distributor in your country *(see last page of the book for addresses).*

Prices charged at the OECD Bookshop.

THE OECD CATALOGUE OF PUBLICATIONS and supplements will be sent free of charge
on request addressed either to OECD Publications Service,
or to the OECD Distributor in your country.

TABLE OF CONTENTS

Preface 7

COUNTRY SUMMARIES

Australia 9
Austria 13
Belgium 16
Canada 18
Denmark 20
Finland 21
France 23
Germany 26
Greece 27
Ireland 28
Italy 30
Japan 31
Luxembourg 33
Netherlands 35
New Zealand 36
Norway 39
Portugal 41
Spain 43
Sweden 53
Switzerland 58
Turkey 61
United Kingdom 63
United States 64

Annex I.　　LIST OF NATIONAL CORRESPONDENTS 67

Annex II.　　STATISTICS 69

PREFACE

This series of reports is designed to meet the growing demand in both Member and non-Member countries for up-to-date information on the policies, programmes and measures being undertaken to improve the efficiency and effectiveness of public sector management. These reports put into a succinct, easily accessible form a large amount of dispersed information in an emerging area of structural adjustment policy.

The current report, as its name implies, updates the information contained in the 1990 Survey publication. It should, therefore, be read in association with that publication which provides the context for many of the initiatives mentioned in the present report. For this reason, the format remains similar, i.e. a set of country summaries provided by national correspondents, a list of those contacts, and a selection of statistical tables on the government sector extracted from existing OECD sources.

Correspondents in 23 Member countries have contributed to the present report, including Austria and Luxembourg which were not covered in the 1990 Survey. The material submitted indicates that some significant initiatives were developed during 1990 in a number of Member countries. Salient examples include: the *Administration Management Project* in Austria; the *White Paper on the Renewal of the Public Service* in Canada; the *Renewal of the Public Service* initiative in France; *Large and Small-Scale Efficiency Operations* in the Netherlands; a *National Day for Debureaucratisation* in Portugal; the comprehensive *Modernisation Plan* in Spain; and the *Management Control Project* in Switzerland.

At the same time it is possible, in all countries, to detect continuity in the reform policy agenda as identified in the 1990 Survey. There has also been structural re-organisation aimed at improving the co-ordination and implementation of policy. In some cases, restructuring has involved experiments with a new division of responsibilities between the public and private sectors, and elsewhere with a more intensive scrutiny of the division of tasks between different levels of government. Much emphasis continues to be placed in all countries on improving the management of human resources and on re-aligning financial management systems to focus more on the results and outputs of government activities, and on how these may best be measured.

AUSTRALIA

Management of Human Resources

Performance appraisal programmes for the Senior Executive Service are now in place in most departments and agencies. Programmes are the responsibility of individual departments and agencies, and are to be developed having regard to guidelines issued by the Public Service Commission (PSC). Programmes are only to be used for performance pay where endorsed by the PSC. Extension of performance appraisal and pay to the Senior Officer group is under consideration by the Industrial Relations Commission.

A *Joint Australian Public Service Training Council* has been set up. It comprises representatives from unions and departments. It has put in hand extensive project work related to development of competencies across the Australian Public Service (APS) as the prelude to development of a new training infrastructure for the APS. The Commonwealth, pursuant to the Middle Management Development initiative, and the States have set up a joint venture to develop a public sector management course for middle managers across Australia. Pilot courses are to be delivered in late 1991.

The Joint APS Training Council met for the first time on 3-4 September 1990. The key functions of the Council are to advise on:

— the establishment of parameters for the conduct of skills audits of existing and future skill requirements and resulting training needs;

— the development of APS-wide priorities such as the development of core competencies and related training standards, competency-based assessment, curriculum development and accredited training programmes;

— changes to existing training programmes required to meet skill formation and skill formation requirements;

— the facilitation of skills recognition, accreditation and articulation of on-the-job and off-the-job training in the APS, including through liaising with outside training providers; and identification of innovative training responses including specific Structural Efficiency Principle initiatives with APS-wide potential which will improve the level, quality and flexibility of training in the APS.

The recent survey on *human resources development* (HRD) in the APS indicates that increased resources are being devoted to HRD and there is a continuing move towards a more strategic focus in HRD activity.

Developments in the Australian Public Service

Significant improvements have been made in the areas of hours of duty (ordinary duty, overtime and shiftwork), allowances for staff required to be available for duty outside normal working hours, and Award amalgamations. There is now a greater span of "ordinary duty" (non-overtime) hours. Overtime provisions for administrative staff have been brought closer to the industry standard, and new shiftwork provisions provide scope for greater flexibility in working arrangements. There is agreement that the structure of payments for staff required to be available for duty outside ordinary hours has been simplified. The coverage of industrial Awards covering public servants is being simplified with 23 Awards covering professional staff being amalgamated into two, and other Award amalgamations are well advanced.

Non-Public Service Act Areas of Commonwealth Employment

In 1987 the Government announced a package of reforms to the transport and communications *Government Business Enterprises* (GBEs) with the intention of improving their performance by replacing detailed controls with accountability. This represented a significant change in emphasis particularly in the area of industrial relations co-ordination.

The previous arrangements required enterprises to consult with the Department of Industrial Relations on a wide range of issues from major wages and conditions matters to initiatives on occupational health and safety and industrial democracy. The new arrangements allowed greatly increased responsibility and autonomy within standard guidelines on government wages and industrial policy, established by the Minister for Industrial Relations.

During 1990, working within these guidelines, most Statutory Authorities and GBEs have achieved substantial progress in implementing meaningful changes as a result of agreements developed under the structural efficiency principles. Changes have involved new classification structures; advancement within classifications and structures based on skill acquisition rather than age and years of service; and more flexible working arrangements involving multi-skilling and working hours.

Changes have also occurred in the process for setting GBE *executive remuneration*. Prior to the revised arrangements, salary and allowances for the Chief Executive Officer (CEO) of a GBE were set by the Remuneration Tribunal leading to a broad but inappropriate alignment with salaries and allowances within the Australian Public Service. The new arrangements allow the Boards of the various enterprises to determine the remuneration of the Chief Executive in consultation with the Tribunal, taking into account remuneration arrangements applicable in relevant areas of the commercial sector. The remuneration established by this process for the CEO effectively forms the cap for other executives within the enterprise. In return for more commercially competitive remuneration, GBE executives have had to forego tenure, and all positions are re-advertised both within Australia and overseas and appointments made on the basis of merit.

Budgetary Reform and Financial Management

As part of the programme of reform in government purchasing, a major service-wide study of training needs was undertaken in 1989/90. As a result, the Department of Administrative Services has established a *Purchasing Development Centre* to be the prime mover in staff development and training.

The Senate Committee on Finance and Public Administration has conducted a three-part enquiry into the format and content of Commonwealth agencies' Explanatory Notes, processes for the scrutiny of Special/Standing Appropriations, and the operations of Trust Funds within the Commonwealth Public Account. The Committee's findings are expected to be published soon and enhance accountability to Parliament.

The *Social Justice Strategy* of the Government seeks to incorporate social justice concerns into Programme Management and Budgeting systems by requiring programme managers across the APS to adopt approaches which will enhance the social effectiveness of their programmes. This includes the identification of social justice objectives for programmes and their reflection in programme development and implementation as well as the collection of statistics and other data for the purpose of monitoring the impact of programmes.

Progress towards the incorporation of this approach is monitored annually by the Social Justice Secretariat (within the Department of the Prime Minister and Cabinet), largely through the examination of portfolio Explanatory Notes and Annual Reports.

The Federal Government's *Access and Equity Strategy* (AES) is aimed at ensuring that the design and delivery of government programmes and services takes into account the different racial, cultural and linguistic backgrounds of clients. Australia is a multi-cultural society and resources are wasted if government programmes and services do not take account of this fact. A revised strategy was launched in 1989/90 which requires portfolio agencies to, *inter alia:*

- review, monitor and evaluate all services and programmes and policies to take account of that diversity;
- implement ethnicity data guidelines;
- deliver services and implement programmes in languages other than English, when necessary;
- sensitise policy development and service delivery staff to this diversity;
- allow opportunities for participation by members of the various cultural, linguistic and racial groups in policy formulation and in improving programme and service delivery;
- develop appropriate information programmes and consultative mechanisms;
- publish three-year AES plans;
- consider programme implementation of the AES in both internal and external audits; and,
- include an Access and Equity section in Annual Reports.

The Office of Multi-cultural Affairs within the Department of the Prime Minister and Cabinet has responsibility for both monitoring implementation of and developing the AES.

Project Monitoring and Evaluation

In 1988, the Government endorsed a strategy to improve the quality of programme evaluation in the APS. One key element was the development by agencies of three-year portfolio evaluation plans, reviewed on an annual basis. During 1990/91, the Department of Finance plans to develop a small information system that will aid in determining the coverage of these plans and in monitoring the quality and management of significant programme evaluations undertaken by each portfolio. Also, following a Cabinet Submission in 1990, agencies will be required to publicise and circulate the results of major evaluations of certain programmes which can be made public without compromising confidentiality of sensitive information or information which could impact on national security.

The Australian National Audit Office is presently undertaking an efficiency audit into evaluation.

Institutional Responsibility for Public Management Reform

The status of the Government's *Financial Management Improvement Programme* (FMIP) has been evaluated by the House of Representatives Standing Committee on Finance and Public Administration and a report tabled in Parliament. The enquiry found that despite progress made in Programme Management and Budgeting by agencies, a more "concentrated effort to develop performance information, management information, reporting systems and evaluation planning processes" should be made. The FMIP will be comprehensively evaluated in 1992.

Much significant work is being undertaken by the *Management Improvement Advisory Committee* (MIAC). A major report on Asset Management was presented in 1990. Other projects include one on performance measurement and evaluation and others on devolution and accountability.

A *Special Premiers' Conference* was held in October 1990 between federal and state leaders to agree on a co-operative effort to "help make Australia more efficient and competitive". This will be achieved in part by reducing duplication and negotiating greater commonality of objectives between federal and state issues. A further special meeting will be held in May 1991 to assess progress made in this area.

Amendments to the text on Australia in the 1990 Survey:

— On page 19, delete the following from the end of the second paragraph: "... and in legislative action which continues today."

— On page 20, add the following to the second paragraph, line 4: "... and retirement, Equal Employment Opportunity, Senior Executive Service and Human Resource Development."

— On page 20, add the following to the second paragraph, after the fourth sentence: "The Merit Protection and Review Agency (MPRA) was established on 1 July 1985 as an independent authority; its creation was designed to remove any potential for conflict between the role of the (then) Public Service Board as an appeal body and its role as principal employing authority."

— On page 20, add the following to the end of the fifth paragraph: "Further efforts to develop improved management information systems and performance indicators are continuing."

— On page 21, add the following to the end of the fourth paragraph:

"— the requirement under the Training Guarantee legislation that employers, including public sector employers, fulfil a minimum training obligation."

— On page 21, replace the last word in the sixth paragraph with "1991".

— On page 23, replace the fifth paragraph with the following:

"Revised regulations covering purchasing were introduced in November 1990 and established value for money as the objective of government purchasing, and open and effective competition as the means of achieving it. Practical guidance for purchasing agencies is being provided progressively. The main vehicle for this purpose is the series of Commonwealth Procurement Guidelines issued by the Minister for Administrative Services under the Audit Act 1901. Additional advice on sound purchasing practices is provided in handbooks and administrative circulars."

— On page 24, in the sixth paragraph, line 5, replace "(MAB — see above)" with: "which is chaired by the head of the Department of the Prime Minister and Cabinet."

AUSTRIA

Most of the management development programmes in Austria are currently being drafted within the context of the *"Administration Management Project"*. On the basis of the decision of the Council of Ministers of 3 May 1988, the aims of the Administration Management Project may be summarised as follows:

— *Tightening up the task and management* structure of the public service through concentrating efforts on the core tasks in order to ensure that these are performed.

— *Increasing productivity* in the administration by 20 per cent over the next four years through improving the balance between financial and personnel inputs on one side and the service performance of the public administration on the other.

— *Reducing the cost of administrative activity* through greater use of cost and performance data in decision-making.

— *Concentration on management tasks.*

— *More balanced division of labour for public administration employees.*

— A more *citizen-oriented administration* by stepping up the *service function,* providing the citizen with more rapid and qualitatively better decision-making and reducing costs of the service provided.

— *Preservation of the sovereignty of the department* by implementing the project within the department.

The Administration Management Project was launched in January 1989 in accordance with a decision taken by the Council of Ministers on 20 December 1988. It has four phases:

— Phase One: preliminary analysis to find solutions to simple problems and to define the problems needing in-depth analysis.

— Phase Two: implementing Phase One solutions and doing in-depth analysis (both interdepartmental and intradepartmental).

— Phase Three: implementing proposed Phase Two solutions.

— Phase Four: evaluation of results.

A Co-ordinating Committee and a Steering Group have been set up mainly to examine the requirements of a common methodology, the organisation of problem solving for problems extending beyond one department, and the evaluation of proposals.

Summary of Results of Phase One

Phase One was introduced in 13 departments but kept intentionally brief. It provided an opportunity to *assess* the methods and performance quality of external consultancy firms and to react accordingly. Once completed, it was evaluated through individual departmental reports and an overall report addressed to the federal government. Eight different consultancy firms analysed the 13 federal departments and came up with 3 696 proposals. After streamlining and testing for applicability, 2 042 suggestions were retained. Of these, a total of 383 had been implemented in the departments by 15 June 1990. This corresponds to the envisaged productivity increase potential of some 20 per cent.

Of the proposals retained:

— 36 per cent question the tasks of administration (in terms of scope, effectiveness, implementation);

— 41 per cent refer to an improvement in the structural and operational organisation of administration (e.g. competences);

— 18 per cent include demands for improvements in information technology and personal working environment;

— 19 per cent concern management, motivation, remuneration, pre-service and in-service training;

— and 9 per cent can be implemented only in conjunction with legal amendments.

Implementation teams have now been established in all departments under the direction of the project co-ordinator. These teams are to prepare implementation and finance plans; cater to the implementation of practicable proposals; and work on those detailed proposals that can be implemented without external consultants. It is planned that by March 1991, an interim report will be submitted to the federal government on work in progress and results of Phases One and Two. Approximately Sch 40 000 000 have been spent on the project in 1990 on external know-how and consultancy services.

Evaluation of Phase One led to the following list of interdepartmental studies for in-depth analysis:

— reduction of overlapping competences between departments;

— management and personnel;

— budgeting and controlling;

— guidelines for information technology;

— space utilisation scheme for the central federal administration;

— clerical system, technical communication and documentation;

— public relations;

— government procurement;

— approval of and accounting for official journeys.

In-depth Study Groups

Questions of management development are being dealt with by two interdepartmental in-depth study groups: *"Management and Personnel"* and *"Budgeting and Controlling"*. The project group on Management and Personnel decided on five sub-projects which were mainly executed with the assistance of external consultants. The main proposals of the group's report may be summarised as follows:

— *System of job descriptions and evaluations for the entire federal administration.*

— *Personnel selection:* general decentralisation of personnel recruitment and personnel selection (interdepartmental staff selection commissions); central clearing house (Job Exchange) for the entire labour market.

— *On-the-job training for new entrants:* post-entry training on three levels (general knowledge of administration matters, professional skills for the performance of future tasks, personal development) by a mentor system and job rotation; six-month time of introduction; introduction jointly organised by the department concerned and the Human Resources Department.

— *New post-entry basic training:* on-the-job and off-the-job training designed to be complementary; training immediately after entry into the civil service; post-entry basic training disassociated from the official civil service examination; more emphasis on basic and further training in social and communication skills as opposed to professional training.

— *Personnel development concept:* experts in personnel development shall be introduced in all departments; linkage of strategic objectives in the various departments and personnel development; training for executives as they are mainly responsible for personnel development; project pool for managing change.

— *Performance review:* performance reviews are based on agreement of objectives and periodic talks with co-workers; performance level affects further career development as well as pay.

— *Executive officers in central agencies:* career pattern (introduction stage, specialised assignments, phase of generalist and cross-sectional training, permanent job rotation); periodic assessment of management qualities by supervisions and the Human Resources Department.

— *Selection of executive officers:* job description and clearly defined job specifications; internal and external advertisement of all executive positions, placement over a Job Exchange; utilisation of approved selection methods depending on the position to be filled.

— *Management principles for central authorities:* on the basis of mobility, people-centred style of leadership, responsibility of leadership, and responsibility for action; concrete management principles drafted by an interdepartmental working group.

— *Co-determination of the Federal Chancellery and the Federal Ministry of Finance in the human resources management of all departments.* Only 40 co-determination rights out of 100 shall remain.

A first draft report of the Budgeting and Controlling project group has also been prepared. Its main points are:

— Concrete plans to integrate institutional controlling in the various departments.

— A concept for the application of evaluation methods for the administration, based on Anglo-American experiences.

— A concept for the determination of follow-up costs and cost accounting for the federal administration.

— Streamlining and simplification of the Ministry of Finance's co-determination rights in budgetary matters.

Lessons Learned

As at February 1991, Phase Two of the Administration Management Project has been nearly finalised, and Phase Three is ready to be started. The experiences of Phases One and Two can roughly be summarised as follows:

— There is greater readiness for change and renewal among the members of the civil service than expected.

— Adequate political support by the respective Federal Minister responsible for the implementation is an absolute necessity.

— Clear objectives and priorities contribute considerably to the execution of the project as well as to the evaluation and implementation of results.

— Ample time must be available for people working on the project (short-term and comprehensive release from duties for a fixed period of time contributes to the attainment of project objectives).

— The project operative management must be well equipped (staff, budget, electronic data processing).

— Timely information of as many people concerned as possible increases the acceptance of the overall project.

— Special promotion and the use of all supportive elements contribute to the success of the project.

BELGIUM

A law has gone into effect regarding the autonomy and accountability of public enterprises (described in its preliminary phase in the 1990 Survey). Management contracts will be drawn up between the political authorities and the management of the enterprises.

Management of Human Resources

As regards analysis of personnel requirements:

— the individual appropriations for *recruitment* in 1991 have been held at the same level, i.e. set at 1.75 per cent of total staff numbers, with an interdepartmental quota for supplementary appropriation (0.25 per cent) to cover any unexpected additional requirements (e.g. the creation of a new service);

— in 1990 the Permanent Secretariat for Recruitment modernised its *selection techniques,* placing greater emphasis on the non-academic side of the procedure (recruitment of personnel selection consultants), so as to be able to meet the specific job profile requirements of "customer" ministries and agencies;

— the government has given the go-ahead for a project providing for an *in-depth study of personnel requirements,* and work on this began on 1 December 1990. The plan is for each department to acquire the ability to draw up its own organisation chart, taking into account:

  i) changes in tasks, in clientele and in the requirements of that clientele;
  ii) changes in the jobs available on the labour market or in the skills called for by modern management methods;
  iii) changes due to modern information technology and the potential productivity gains resulting from them.

The ultimate aim of the project is that each department should be able to carry out self-assessment and evaluate its own performance on an ongoing basis. It should also allow for a yearly review of personnel requirements taking into consideration both skills and numbers of staff, so that the present system of individual appropriations for recruitment on a linear basis can be eliminated. Such a review might take the form of an annual report on activities.

The management tool involving *master training plans* ("schémas directeurs de formation") was applied for the first time in 1990 according to a method proposed by the civil service authorities. 212 plans were suggested, of which 61 were selected. Experience has shown that the idea is on the whole well received as a means of increasing accountability, but that further thought needs to be given to gearing training to management needs. Appropriations for training staff belonging to all the ministries and administrative agencies for which the Treasury is directly responsible were increased by BF 65 million.

The role of *Civil Service Counsell*ors was redefined in a Royal Decree published on 1 August 1990. It involves only consultancy, providing advice on organisation and personnel management to any ministry or agency that requests it. The government can thus draw on organisational expertise within the civil service.

Several ministries and agencies have already called on the team of Counsellors to make recommendations whose content is revealed only to the managers concerned. The team is also responsible for devising the methodological tool to be used by departments for the purposes of the planned in-depth study of personnel requirements.

Budgetary Reform and Financial Management

A working party has been set up by the Minister of the Budget to consider a plan to introduce zero base budgeting techniques in ministries.

Supplementary Reference Material

LEGRAND, Jean Jacques (1990), "L'Approche belge de la modernisation des administrations publiques : les cellules de modernisation comme outil stratégique de changement", *Administration publique. Revue du droit public et de science administrative,* Bruxelles, T 2-3/1990 (French text only).

Amendments to the text on Belgium in the 1990 Survey:

On page 29, under Section V., change the second sentence of the second paragraph to read as follows:

"In the Ministry of the Civil Service, the General Administration Service and the General Directorate for Selection and Training are responsible, respectively, for all matters concerning the organisation of services and the management of the administrative and financial status of personnel on the one hand (Civil Service Counsellors, recruitment appropriations, in-depth studies), and training — particularly management training — on the other (modernisation units, LOGOS, master training plans)."

CANADA

The Public Service 2000 Initiative

The initiative was launched by the Prime Minister in December 1989. Its objectives were primarily to: meet the challenges of the 21st century with confidence; restore public credibility of government institutions; and deliver increased services under continuing restraint.

Under the leadership of the Clerk of the Privy Council, ten task forces were established — composed of some 120 Deputy and Assistant Deputy Ministers and senior officials — to review essential functions in the Public Service such as training, staffing and classification. In the summer of 1990, the task forces released their reports which included some 300 recommendations.

In December 1990, a year exactly after the launch of PS 2000, the Government released its *White Paper* to guide the Public Service in the year 2000 and beyond. It constitutes a major Government's commitment to improving the quality of service to Canadians provided by the Public Service. It calls for fundamental change in the way the Public Service does its work while at the same time preserving its essential values of excellence, professionalism and non-partisanship.

The key messages of the White Paper are:

— *Better service* will be achieved through a more open, consultative Public Service. Clear standards of service and consultation guidelines will be developed in the months to come. Surveys of results will be done in selected departments.

— *Innovation and empowerment* will be encouraged in order to achieve a more efficient, productive Public Service.

— *Authority will be decentralised* from central agencies to line departments and from headquarters to the regions where most public servants work (67 per cent). Administrative and financial policies will be reduced and simplified. Pilot projects on operating budgets are being introduced in selected departments in 1991, with full implementation planned for 1993/94. All compulsory common services are being reviewed with a view of making them optional. In 1991, departments will have, for example, direct access to suppliers through automated lists as well as control of some tenant services.

— *The Public Service will be more people-oriented.* Public servants are to be recognised "as assets to be valued and developed".

— A *Management Trainee Programme* was introduced at the end of 1990 to attract top graduates into the Public Service.

— Career mobility will be facilitated through the *Human Resources Development Council* (HRDC, see below) and through deployment (movement of an employee to a position at the same group and level).

— *Training and career development* will be improved at all levels, especially for front-line employees. A five-year training plan is to be developed in 1991 by the Treasury Board. Also, career development will be facilitated by a new occupational structure which will include less occupational groups and the creation of a General Services Group comprising most of the groups now part of the Administrative Support and Administrative and Foreign categories.

— *Employment Equity* efforts will include preferential access to development and training for women and other minority groups, specific programmes to help support staff move into the officer category, and longer pay-back period for pension contributions.

— In the *Management Category,* the number of layers below the position of Deputy Minister is not to exceed three — Assistant Deputy Minister, Director General and Director — notwithstanding that there are five promotional steps. Departments will have to make special efforts in 1991 to de-layer the upper echelons of their organisations. The first two levels of the Category, comprising some 3 000 individuals, are to be amalgamated by 1 April 1991. The Treasury Board is also looking at

creating a parallel stream for professionals and specialists. Performance rewards are to be introduced in the Category to bring the Public Service pay more closely into alignment with the private sector.
— These changes will be supported by increased accountability based on clear objectives. To provide a firm basis for this, the Clerk of the Privy Council is to become the statutory Head of the Public Service. He will be required to report annually to the Prime Minister on the state of the Public Service. Deputies' evaluation will be revamped as part of this process.

Human Resources Development Council

The Human Resources Development Council (HRDC), announced by the President of the Treasury Board on 10 October 1990, will provide corporate leadership and strategic direction for the management and development of human resources in the Public Service. The HRDC will provide a forum for senior Deputy Ministers to set strategic direction and foster consultation and co-ordination among departments and between departments and the central agencies.

The HRDC will identify problems and emerging issues in human resources management and develop strategies to address them. A key role will be to identify the future human resources needs of the Public Service and the means for meeting these. The Council will examine "best practices" and models for human resources management regimes in various types of organisations. Finally, the HRDC will provide advice on all issues relating to management's responsibility for human resources.

The Council intends to meet periodically with representatives of the Public Service bargaining agents to exchange views and share ideas on issues related to the management of human resources.

With this new approach, departments will have a direct hand in setting the strategic direction for all aspects of human resources management in the Public Service. The Council should provide a forum for exchanging ideas, for developing common human resource policies which meet departmental needs, and for giving guidance to central agencies regarding their requirements and feedback on the services being provided. This new emphasis on co-operation and a corporate focus will result in greater cohesiveness in the federal government's approach to human resources development.

Supplementary Reference Material

Government of Canada (1990), *Public Service 2000: The Renewal of the Public Service of Canada* (full report and its synopsis tabled in the House of Commons in December 1990), Ottawa.

DENMARK

In May 1990, the Danish government submitted a review of the modernisation programme for the public sector to the Danish Parliament, as mentioned in the 1990 Survey. On the basis of this evaluation, the government is planning a change of the modernisation and debureaucratisation efforts in the future. In 1990, initiatives have been taken in the areas listed below.

Improving the Delivery of Public Services

The ministries' modernisation efforts will in future years be concentrated on improvements of effectiveness and quality of services and on simplification of legislation and rules. Within each ministerial area, one or more customer-oriented areas will be selected, in which a targeted modernisation effort will be implemented to the benefit of members of the public and companies alike.

Visible goals and criteria of success for the projects will be established in preparation for later evaluation.

In February 1991, the Ministry of Finance will publish a guide on the use of criteria of success and result evaluation as management tools in connection with projects on the development of service and quality.

Management of Human Resources

In June 1990, the Ministry of Finance submitted an introduction of an overall government management policy for the 90s, as reported in the 1990 Survey. The draft contained proposed initiatives in the following areas: development of future managers; selection of managers; evaluation of newly-appointed managers; more equal sex distribution; performance-related pay for managers; policy for long-serving staff.

The Ministry of Finance will take a number of initiatives forming parts of the implementation of management policies, including performance-related pay for managers.

Supplementary Reference Material

Ministry of Finance (1990), *Modernisation of the Public Sector in Denmark* (English translation of *Moderniseringsredegørelse 1990*), Copenhagen.

Ministry of Finance (1990), *Statens Lederpolitik i 90'erne,* Department of Management and Personnel, Copenhagen (Danish text only).

FINLAND

The 1990 Survey remains relatively up-to-date and gives an adequate description of public management developments in Finland. A few additional points are presented below, but only the proposals of the Personnel Committee are detailed.

In April 1990, the Government reported to Parliament on the general outlines of the reform of the public administration. The content of this report is relatively close to the goals, priorities and measures presented in the 1990 Survey. The discussion in Parliament was generally in favour of the direction of the reform proposed by the Government.

Market-type Mechanisms

The Post and Telecommunications and the State Railways started to operate as new types of public enterprise from the beginning of 1990. Along the same lines, the National Civil Aviation Organisation will start as a public enterprise at the beginning of 1991. After these reforms, about one-third of the personnel of the Finnish state will be working in public enterprises.

A project has been launched by the Ministry of Finance to improve public service delivery, experiment with new forms of client orientation, and link the improvement of public services more closely to management by results.

Management of Human Resources

At the end of September 1990, the Personnel Committee submitted its *proposals on the reform of the personnel policy* of the state. The Committee proposed a more active and competitive personnel policy as well as the improvement of the management of human resources. This is considered to be a prerequisite for achieving more effectiveness, service capability, and guidance of cost developments within the state administration.

The Personnel Committee also proposed reform to make the position of civil servants more uniform across the state administration. It also proposed a reform of the pay system to support active and well-motivated performance as well as a new organisation of the negotiations and agreement system. Negotiations would be conducted both at the central level and at the level of the agencies. The purpose of this change is to put an end to the traditional unitary office system of the state.

The comments made by the agencies are generally supportive of the proposals of the Personnel Committee. The aim now is to prepare a programme based on the proposals and on the forthcoming decision (probably in February 1991) by the Government which would be implemented in the period 1991-95.

The *implementation* of the new personnel policies has already started in the Ministry of Finance where organisational changes have been made. The former Department of Wages and Salaries was transformed in 1990 into the Personnel Department, in which are concentrated all strategic personnel matters including development of personnel management, personnel training and development, and management development. After these changes, the Personnel Department can take a full responsibility for the strategic development of the personnel resources within the state administration.

Experiments with the reform of the pay system are continuing. These include a new classification of posts based on each position's requirements and on merit pay and productivity bonus. Experiments with result-oriented budgeting systems are being conducted in both public enterprises and in the agencies. So far the results of these experiments have been positive.

The Government decided in November 1990 to leave unfilled 10 per cent of the posts coming open during 1991. This objective is set in addition to the earlier decision to cut the number of posts by 2 800.

Budgetary Reform and Financial Management

Budgetary and financial management reform has also continued. In the 1991 budget proposal, the running costs of 12 major agencies are budgeted according to a reformed, more result-oriented budget structure. In the 1992 budget proposal, the running costs of about 30 more agencies, and by 1995 all agencies, will be budgeted according to the reformed budget structure.

Several supporting projects have been established to modify budgeting documents, improve financial and managerial accounting, and strengthen ministerial guidance of the agencies. Pension costs and some other cost items which until now have been centrally budgeted will be included in agency costs starting from 1991, thus improving cost-consciousness and the quality of management in the agencies.

Supplementary Reference Material

Government of Finland (1990), *Palvelevampaan hallintoon. Valtioneuvoston selonteko eduskunnalle julkisen hallinnon uudistamisesta* (Towards a More Service-oriented Administration. The Report of the Government to Parliament on the Reform of Public Administration), Helsinki (Finnish text only).

Government of Finland (1990), *Henkilöstöpolitiikan uudistaminen.Henkilöstökomitean mietintö* (The Reform of the Personnel Policy. The Proposal of the Personnel Committee), Helsinki (Finnish text only; an English translation of the summary is available).

FRANCE

In general the period since the 1990 Survey has seen progress in the four areas of implementation, assessment, promotion of awareness, and detailed analysis.

The main lines of the first stage of the policy for the *"renewal of the public service"* were drawn up at a government seminar on 21 September 1989 and a start has been made on their implementation. They have already been the subject of initial assessments, notably at meetings between personnel directors of ministries, and at the second government seminar led by the Prime Minister on 11 June 1990. The policy for the "renewal of the public service" has also involved an extensive campaign to heighten the awareness of the personnel concerned, an essential step if staff are to understand what is involved and support the reform. 29 regional colloquia were therefore organised, ending with a large national meeting held in Paris on 29 and 30 November 1990, in order to bring together those involved in the change.

The government seminar of 11 June 1990 marked the beginning of a second stage with four new priorities: decentralisation of the state administration and closer co-ordination of its local services; updating of budgetary and accounting rules; improvement of executive staff policy; and staff management and improvement of working conditions.

A first overall assessment of the measures taken under the policy for the "renewal of the public service" can be made, and a third government seminar is planned for the first quarter of 1991.

Management of Human Resources

Achievements in the first stage primarily concern the following matters. A Framework Agreement on *continuing training* of state civil servants was signed on 29 June 1989 providing, with a view to manpower planning, for allowance for training in the course of an official's career and preparation of an individual training plan, integration of new techniques and skills, and retraining of the least skilled categories of staff. Negotiations have begun in each ministry and have led to the conclusion of 11 ministerial agreements, with two others under preparation, and the drawing up of five training plans.

On 9 February 1990 a Protocol of Agreement was signed with five trade union organisations providing for renewal of the *scales of skills and remuneration* for the 4.8 million public servants covered. This reform will involve expenditure over seven years of FF 42 billion, and the first implementing measures were adopted on 1 August 1990 after consultation with the signatory bodies. At the same time as raising some salaries, these measures provide for the elimination over two years, by retraining, of the unskilled office worker category (27 000 staff). These provisions also re-organise the careers of some administrative officials (workers or employees), and make provision for a training plan covering the reskilling and transformation of the jobs and functions of 80 000 staff.

Some new measures under the second stage have already been applied. To improve *working conditions,* the legal representative bodies will have their powers extended as defined as part of the negotiations with the trade unions.

Manpower planning will be facilitated by analysis in Autumn 1990 of an extensive statistical survey of staff in all ministries. The method will be tried out for higher executive staff in six ministries. In time, such action will lead to implementation of genuine manpower planning.

The emphasis placed on executive staff policies took material form by the sending of letters to all Ambassadors and local representatives of the state defining their functions. This is to be extended to all directors of the central administration and public establishments of the state. Steps will also be taken to improve information available in ministries on higher executive posts.

Performance, Accountability and Control

The *project management approach,* one of the priorities affirmed by the government at the seminar on 21 September 1989, has been applied in numerous ways. While preparation of national measures is well advanced, some implementing measures at local level have already been taken.

A *"modernisation plan"* has been drawn up in each ministry, as reported in the 1990 Survey.

In each region a *"decentralised government administration project"* has made it possible, under the direction of the representative of the State, to establish a complete diagnosis of the local state administration.

"Service projects", a very innovatory approach, have been adopted by over 200 bodies, ranging from prisons to directorates of the central administration. These projects have already led to redefinition of certain functions and responsibilities, as between the central, regional and departmental levels of the state administration.

In addition, 60 *"centres of accountability"* have been set up since 5 June 1990. They are a more experimental form giving greater autonomy of management, since in exchange for meeting targets expressed in figures, they benefit from more flexible management rules and contractual relations with the central administration. Their autonomy remains subject to application of management control instruments.

The setting up of these last two types of organisation, service projects and centres of accountability, results from the same concern to evaluate action by the administration both internally in relation to personnel, and externally vis-à-vis the public.

Lastly, the government seminar of 11 June 1990 came up with a new idea, namely the *"collective modernisation dividend"*. As the next stage of project management, this entails introducing ways of recognising financially the contribution made by staff to improvements to the efficiency of the administration. The necessary consultation with the trade unions should make it possible to devise some collective, reversible and decentralised mechanism. This should benefit from the effort currently being made by all administrative departments to equip themselves with modern and objective analytical management tools.

At the end of 1990 a report was submitted by the working party responsible for examining the upgrading and use of the experience of staff capable of performing internal consultancy services.

The *assessment* of public policies, the second government priority, began to be implemented with the inauguration by the President of the Republic of the Scientific Evaluation Council and the holding of the first meeting of the Interministerial Evaluation Committee on 26 July 1990. Five themes were examined: the rehabilitation of public housing; the social integration of adolescents with problems; the reception of underprivileged groups by public services; children's school and leisure hours, etc.; and development of data processing and administrative efficiency.

Management of Decision-making and Organisation of Public Services

This is the field in which the last stage of the policy for the "renewal of the public service" is the most innovatory, in the form of the *decentralisation of the state administration.*

Admittedly, previously planned reforms have already been started, such as the globalisation of operating appropriations which will be fully effective under the 1991 Finance Act. However, measures planned in regard to decentralisation are the most ambitious step forward, particularly in the budgetary and financial fields with the decentralisation of a large mass of investment or intervention appropriations. At the same time, management of personnel in the "employee" and "worker" categories will be decentralised as from 1991. 180 decentralisation and regulatory simplification measures have been identified, some of which take effect as from the end of 1990. In addition, procedures are under study to strengthen the co-ordination of local state services in fields such as training and real estate management.

As regards *the organisation of public services,* special mention should be made of the reform of the posts and telecommunications services (PTT) started in Spring 1990. The division of a ministry into two public establishments allows for the better use of resources for two activities which the development of technology and regulations is tending to separate, i.e. the postal and telecommunications services.

Concerning the organisation of the public authorities, mention should first be made of discussion of a government bill to amend the status of Corsica, giving more powers to locally elected bodies to reflect the special features of the island and prepare it for the single market in 1992.

Second, a local administration development bill is under discussion. In addition to greater decentralisation of state services in favour of its representative at the regional level, this provides for more democracy in local life, new forms of co-operation between local authorities (regions or communities), and a defined framework for international co-operation by decentralised authorities.

Supplementary Reference Material (all in French only)

Ministry for the Public Service and Administrative Reform (1990), *Renouveau du service publique. Les rencontres 1990* (Volume I: Sélection des textes officiels; Volume II: Séminaire gouvernemental du 11 juin 1990), les Journaux officiels, Paris.

Ministry for the Public Service and Administrative Reform (1990), *La Fonction publique de l'État en 1989,* (annual report), la Documentation française, Paris.

Ministry for the Public Service and Administrative Reform (1990), *Les Projets de service,* la Documentation française, Paris.

Ministry for the Public Service and Administrative Reform (1990), "Accord-cadre sur la formation continue dans la fonction publique de l'Etat", (brochure), Directorate General for Administration and the Public Service, Paris.

Ministry for the Public Service and Administrative Reform (1990), "La Formation, outil du renouveau", (brochure), Directorate General for Administration and the Public Service, Paris.

Ministry for the Public Service and Administrative Reform (1990), *La rénovation de la grille de la fonction publique,* Prime Minister's Information and Distribution Service (SID), Paris.

International Institute of Public Administration (1990), *L'Année administrative 1989,* Paris.

Cour des comptes (1990), *Annual Report,* Paris.

GERMANY

The division of the two German states ended with the *accession of eastern Germany (German Democratic Republic before the unification of Germany) on 3 October 1990.* Since then, the Länder Brandenburg, Mecklenburg-Western Pomerania, Saxony, Saxony-Anhalt and Thuringia are federated states of Germany (Federal Republic of Germany after the unification of Germany). The 23 boroughs of Berlin form Land Berlin.

Due to the existing rights and responsibilities for the whole of Germany and Berlin reserved by the former war allies, the German unity could only be established in close co-operation and agreement with the former occupation powers. Furthermore, the membership in the European Communities of western Germany (Federal Republic of Germany before the unification of Germany) and the interests of its immediate neighbours had to be taken into account.

Owing to the fact that all parties concerned were continuously involved in the preparations, it was possible to complete this unique achievement — the Unification Treaty — which is unparalleled as regards the extent, diversity and complexity of the regulations contained therein, in such a short time.

One of the basic aims of the Unification Treaty is to ensure that the new Länder and municipalities have the financial capacity to act. This is why the proven financial system of the *Basic Law,* including the regulations concerning joint tasks of the Federal Government and the Länder, has basically been enacted in the new Länder.

According to the Treaty, the capital of Germany shall be Berlin. The seat of the Parliament and Government shall be decided at a later date. Third October shall be a public holiday known as the Day of German Unity.

Specific provisions had to be made on *transitional arrangements for administrative institutions,* the legal status of persons formerly employed in the civil service of eastern Germany, the handing over of public financial assets including the special funds of Deutsche Reichsbahn (railways) and Deutsche Post and public debts. Moreover, it was necessary to pass regulations governing the distribution and winding-up of tasks that had formerly been executed by the central government of eastern Germany. Other specific arrangements were required for institutions in the fields of culture, broadcasting, education, science and sport, which had been under central governmental control in eastern Germany. In addition, the Treaty lays the foundations for establishing federal structures, Land administrations and efficient local governments in the new states.

In view of the enormous *in-service training* needs in the new states, the *Federal Academy for Public Administration* (in the Federal Ministry of the Interior), which is in charge of the Federal Government's central in-service training for members of the civil service of the Länder, offers a variety of in-service training courses.

The Federal Academy provides five weeks of basic courses for members of the higher service of the former east German administration who are to be taken over into the federal civil service. The course is to give an introduction to the constitutional order of the Basic Law and the guiding principles of administration and management in a democratic and federal state under the rule of law, thereby taking into account the basic structures of social market economy.

The Federal Academy is prepared to support the organisation of training courses and, if need be, the establishment of new in-service training institutions in the new Länder by means of providing commissioners or other officials in charge of in-service training with appropriate training. It is planned to hold pilot courses in the new federal states from Spring 1991 onwards.

GREECE

The main policy goals of the Greek Government have been strongly centred during this period around economic improvement and development, while a series of measures has been taken towards the modernisation of the internal functioning of the administration in general.

The public sector was redefined and reduced to a "more effective" area by the *Law 1892/1990*. In this context, the major programme of privatisation of public enterprises characterised as "problematic" deserves mention again.

General directorates have been established (positions and grades) in ministries and other public bodies so as to improve co-ordination of the services provided. Units of strategic planning analysis and evaluation of public policy have also been established in the ministries.

The need for signatures on administrative documents has been reduced. This has simplified procedures, made services more productive (by a vast delegation of authority), and improved relations between the administration and citizens.

The participation of public servants in programmes of training, re-education or specialisation has been defined as obligatory in career development. A reward system has been established for civil servants who propose measures and ideas for improving organisation of work, simplification of procedures, modernisation of methods, etc.

A body of controllers of public administration, established by a previous *Law (1735/1987)* in the Ministry to the Presidency of Government, is to become responsible for cases of accusations and complaints of citizens against the administration. By a ministerial act of the same Ministry, Inspection Units are also to be established in the ministries to follow up on the administrative action. And, by *Law 1884/1990,* a judicial functionary now presides over the service councils which deal with selection for supervisory positions.

Finally, the Government is continuing in its effort towards developing a more strategic and integrated approach to human resource management by controlling personnel entry into the public sector in general.

IRELAND

Relocation of Sections of Central Government Departments

In 1987, the Government announced a programme for the decentralisation to twelve regional centres of up to 3 000 civil servants then based in Dublin. Moves involving some 1 200 of the total took place in 1989/90. A further 1 200 staff are due for transfer in 1991/92, but there have been difficulties (due in part to the successful reduction of civil service numbers) in identifying suitable groups to make up the balance. However, it is still intended to identify suitable sections (if necessary from the broader Public Service) and to implement their transfer as soon as practicable.

Improving the Delivery of Public Services

A survey of public offices was carried out by the Department of Finance in 1989/90 to ascertain the extent to which such offices guaranteed adequate standards of privacy for members of the public wishing to transact business of a personal or confidential nature.

The results of the survey showed that, in general, public offices are providing a reasonable standard of privacy. Some areas where improvements are desirable were identified. The situation will continue to be reviewed.

The survey also showed that departments are conscious of the need for suitable training for staff assigned to public offices and that this is being provided on an ongoing basis.

Budgetary Reform and Financial Management

The Government decided that the system of delegated administrative budgets should apply in all government departments as from 1 March 1991. These budgets, which cover all administrative costs (such as pay, information technology and accommodation) are fixed for the years up to and including 1993, and incorporate a 2 per cent annual reduction in real terms. Within the budget limits, heads of departments have considerable discretion in the use of resources without requiring the approval of the Department of Finance. Departments are expected to carry the process of delegating budgets through to their own line managers.

Management of Human Resources

The embargo on recruitment concerning the entire public service was introduced in 1987. In 1990, the filling of essential posts has been authorised, subject to the approval of the Minister for Finance. In the 1991 Budget, the Minister for Finance stated that the consolidation of the reduction in staff numbers — achieved through the embargo on recruitment and an early retirement scheme — will continue, and there will be no general resumption in public service recruitment.

A major initiative in 1990 was the introduction of a performance-related pay scheme for the Assistant Secretary grade (i.e. the general second-level echelon in the top management hierarchy). The scheme replaced the traditional incremental pay scale with a pay range, the speed of progression through which is determined by reference to assessed performance. Performance is assessed on a preceding-year basis and, as far as possible, is based on achievement of agreed objectives/results. The scheme was introduced consequent on recommendations contained in a report of an independent review body (Report No. 30 of the Review Body on Higher Remuneration in the Public Sector, 1987). Similar performance-related pay schemes were recommended and authorised for the chief executives of commercial state-sponsored bodies.

Introduction and Use of Information Technology

In the drive to improve performance in terms of efficiency and effectiveness, the use of information technology continues to expand. As in previous years, particular emphasis has been attached to infrastructural developments. The country-wide Government Telecommunications Network (GTN) was officially launched in June 1990 and is now scheduled to be completed by end 1992. The GTN is an integrated voice and data network designed to provide efficient and cost-effective communications and to support the current decentralisation programme.

A further development was the launching of a pilot X.400 message handling system linking five departments, including the Office of the Irish Permanent Representation to the European Communities in Brussels. The system was of considerable benefit during the Irish Presidency of the EC in the first half of 1990.

On the personnel front, a new payment by way of an annual gratuity has been introduced for certain staff engaged full-time in IT work and who possess high-level skills/expertise essential to the performance of their work. The new payments are designed to help retain highly skilled IT staff longer in the civil service.

Productivity and Efficiency Measurement

The Efficiency Audit Group which was established by the Government set up a working party in 1990 to carry out a review of the Department of Defence, which is expected to report in January 1991. The Group is presently initiating detailed reviews of other Government departments.

Supplementary Reference Material

Review Body on Higher Remuneration in the Public Sector (1987), *Report No. 30 to the Minister for Finance on the Levels of Remuneration appropriate to Higher Posts in the Public Sector,* Dublin.

ITALY

For 1990, mention should be made of the latest edition of the *Report to Parliament on the status of the public administration,* in particular concerning the experience gained in Italy through the project known as "Functionality and Efficiency of the Public Administration" (FEPA); and changes of an *organisational nature,* such as those in the following 1990 laws:

— "Modifications concerning offences by public officials against the public administration" (Law No. 86, 26 April);

— "Code of local autonomy" (Law No. 142, 8 June);

— "Regulations governing the right to strike in essential public services" (Law No. 146, 12 June);

— "New standards in matters of administrative procedure and the right of access to administrative documents" (Law No. 241, 7 August).

Laws 86/1990 and 241/1990 complement one another to some extent, but the latter innovates with respect to the need for *proper relations between the public administration and the citizen,* and *uniformity in the essential characteristics of administrative procedures,* all aimed at meeting criteria of economy, efficiency and transparency. Especially worthy of note are the issues of identifying responsibilities for administrative procedures, participation of citizens in those procedures, simplification of the procedures through co-ordination meetings and less strict deadlines and procedures for consultative activities, and rules for administrative documentation including access rights and administrative secrecy.

The laws on local autonomy and on the right to strike are of a more institutional character. The first is aimed at revitalising *effective co-operation between regions, communes and provinces* in their respective fields of competence. This implies on an administrative level that, to guarantee the regularity and legality of local authority action, an official opinion should be sought even if it is not binding. Similarly, the notion of a clear distinction between political and administrative responsibility emerges as important, and underlies the philosophy behind the reform of the senior civil service currently being studied by Parliament.

Law 146/1990 sets a standard for deciding between different fundamental rights provided for and protected under the Constitution in such cases where conflict should arise between them. This law is not only a first application of Article 39 of the Constitution on the right to strike, but also a method in its own right for a *correct and modern reading of the Constitution.* It introduces a right of general validity — in this case, the right to strike — in the context of other rights guaranteed under the Constitution and therefore to be protected. The law arises out of what has happened in recent years because of the intensification of conflicts in the public sector, where exercising the right to strike has led to infringements of the basic rights of third parties completely outside the conflict itself.

The legislator thus coined the notion of *"essential public services"*, thereby allowing the right to strike and other similarly protected rights to co-exist; and requested that the identification of essential services, and the definition of clauses concerning the rules, measures and procedures governing the delivery of them, be negotiated with the unions. The violation of such rules, measures and procedures, like the violation of legal provisions, is now subject to administrative sanction.

It should also be mentioned that the issue of *citizen-administration relations* has been the main thrust of the contractual reforms. These included the establishment of public relations offices, identification badges for public officials, vocational training for civil servants aimed at improving relations with clients, simplification and standardisation of official forms, extension of office opening hours, reinforcement and co-ordination of computer links between administrations, and improvement of the logistics dedicated to client service.

There is also a phenomenon of institutionalisation (even if presently in the initial stages) of *client associations* which are already being recognised in establishing client-administration relations. Also, in the strategic development of local health services, commissions for checking and reviewing service quality and health provision have consulted "experts". This subject could be examined more deeply as the key factor in the articulation of political and administrative responsibilities.

JAPAN

The Provisional Commission for Administrative Reform, set up by specific establishment law in 1981, is an advisory council to the Prime Minister. It has set objectives for administrative reform in Japan, as reported in the 1990 Survey. To oversee the implementation of the reform, a Provisional Council for the Promotion of Administrative Reform was established for a three-year term in 1983. A second Council was established in 1987 for another three years. The third Provisional Council for the Promotion of Administrative Reform was established in October 1990 for another three-year term.

Organisational Changes

Legislation on the organisation of ministries and agencies has been changed to reduce legislative control over organisational arrangements and to facilitate flexible and swift organisational changes. The aim of re-organising or abolishing 10 per cent of all divisions and equivalent units below bureau or department level by the end of 1988 has been completely achieved.

Reducing the Share of the Public Sector

The privatisation of three major public corporations has been implemented: the Japanese National Railways, the Nippon Telegraph and Telephone Public Corporation, and the Japan Tobacco and Salt Public Corporation. The division and privatisation of the former Japanese National Railways into several passenger railways and a country-wide freight railway has revitalised the business with better service. The privatisation of the Nippon Telegraph and Telephone Public Corporation, together with the deregulation of the telecommunications industry, has stimulated competition and led to the development of new and better services. Measures to abolish or consolidate, privatise and rationalise functions of other public corporations have also been taken.

Management of Human Resources

The size of the workforce of the national government is strictly controlled by the *Total Staff Number Law* which sets the "ceiling" of the number of full-time employees of the national government as a whole. Within the limit of this ceiling, human resources are re-allocated among ministries and agencies by means of an annual review of requests to meet new and/or increased demands or workloads and planned reduction of personnel.

On the basis of *personnel reduction plans* since 1968, the seventh personnel reduction plan was decided upon by the Cabinet in 1986. This decision set a target of a 5 per cent reduction in the number of civil servants of the national government within five years from 1987. In view of the necessity and possibility of reduction, the ratio of reduction was differentiated from ministry to ministry.

Management of Regulatory Review and Reform

Efforts to eliminate and curtail regulations to lessen the administrative burden on the citizen and diminish bureaucracy have continued. Deregulation or regulatory reform efforts have been made in many fields such as distribution, transportation, telecommunications, finance, energy, agricultural products, inspection, testing, qualification systems, etc.

Project Monitoring and Evaluation

The Administrative Management Bureau of the Management and Co-ordination Agency, as a centre for the promotion of administrative reform, monitors the progress of reform programmes. The Administrative Inspection Bureau of the same Agency also conducts inspections of reform efforts of ministries and agencies concerned.

Institutional Responsibility for Public Management Reform

— Prime Minister's Office (Management and Co-ordination Agency)
— Cabinet Secretariat
— Ministry of Finance
— Ministry of Home Affairs
— National Personnel Authority

The *Management and Co-ordination Agency* was set up in 1984 to strengthen central managerial functions and to play a government-wide co-ordinating role effectively for several substantive policy areas: personnel management; management of organisation of government agencies (including public corporations) and control of manpower; inspection of operations of government agencies and programmes; statistical standards and statistical surveys; pensions. This Agency follows up the implementation of the Provisional Commission reports.

The *Cabinet Secretariat* has the co-ordination function for government policy. There are two sections dealing respectively with domestic policy and external policy.

The *Ministry of Finance* is responsible for the preparation of the annual budget of the government.

The *Ministry of Home Affairs* is in charge of administrative and financial systems (including tax) of local government.

The *National Personnel Authority* was set up to ensure the fair operations of personnel management and is in charge of, among other things, remuneration, recruitment, training, and working conditions. This agency is a highly independent organisation under the jurisdiction of the Cabinet.

LUXEMBOURG

Like its neighbours, the Luxembourg public administration is currently faced with a whole series of problems, the most important of which may be briefly summed up as follows.

Recruitment

The Luxembourg administration is experiencing serious recruitment problems at the moment in such careers as junior executive officer and the teaching profession, and in technical careers such as engineering. These recruitment difficulties are due in part to the fierce competition on the employment market because of the boom in the service sector and also because some candidates for public employment are put off by the inflexibility of the administrative system and above all by the numerous examinations that have to be taken.

Staff Training

The creation of the *Administrative Training Institute* in 1983 finally filled the long-lasting vacuum in the area of initial and continuing training of public servants in the major careers in most public departments. The great success of the Institute's activities has prompted those in charge to undertake a comprehensive reform of the present system in order to give still more public servants the opportunity to improve their professional knowledge.

Career Development

The current system of career development is dominated by promotion on the basis of seniority. Legislation in 1986 emphasised automatic promotion in the civil service after a number of years in the lower grades. Access to the higher grades depends on the marks obtained in an examination which determines the permanent ranking of those concerned. It is only in the last career grade that the head of administration assesses the merits of each candidate (supported by proof of continuing in-service training and of the need to fill a post with particular responsibilities). One of the most pressing reforms in the coming years will be to improve the performance of public servants by making greater use of appraisals of the quality of the work of each official.

Computerisation

In contrast to the initial centralisation of the administration's computer services through the creation of the State Computer Centre and following an *ad hoc* study by a private company, the aim of government policy at present is to equip all public services with essential office automation facilities and hence to promote optimum management of their human and material resources.

Reform of the Administration

The administrative structure is still mainly characterised by excessive rigidity due largely to the rules of administrative law on which it is based. The administration must be more receptive to the public by making a number of reforms concerning information for citizens, the handling of their cases, and pre-contentious and contentious procedures. It goes without saying that many of these changes will require new legislation.

Free Movement of Workers

The principle of the free movement of workers in Europe is bound to create problems when applied to the civil service. The difficulties are partly due to the service conditions of public servants, which comprise reciprocal rights and duties flowing from the nationality requirement laid down by the Constitution and current legislation. The administration also has a very important part to play in the exercise of public authority and in protecting the general interests of the state. So, while pointing out the degree of free movement of workers already achieved in the Grand Duchy and not ruling out constructive future dialogue with the European Communities, the Luxembourg Government is not for the moment considering any additional measures to promote the free movement of workers so far as public administration is concerned.

NETHERLANDS

The Dutch Government has started two major operations aiming at improving efficiency and effectiveness of the public sector. Both operations start effectively in 1991.

First, there is the so-called *large-scale efficiency operation.* The central elements of this operation are reduction of government tasks and improvement of the structure of organisation. This structural improvement can take different forms: decentralisation of tasks to local government; functional decentralisation (by forming relatively independent agencies); deregulation; privatisation; elimination of double work; efficiency improvement by using information technology.

A Ministerial Committee has been formed to steer the operation. The secretaries-general of the ministries have been instructed to generate proposals. The Government will make decisions on these proposals in the Spring of 1991.

In addition to the general aims as mentioned above, the Government has also set a financial target for the large-scale efficiency operation. By 1994, the operation must result in a structural cost-reduction of 300 million guilders.

Second, there is the *small-scale efficiency operation.* This operation aims at enhancing labour productivity in the public sector by 0.5 per cent per year using, among others, technological developments such as computerisation. The idea behind this operation is that it is thought possible to increase productivity in the public sector by the same percentage as is realised in comparable private sector activities.

NEW ZEALAND

Market-type Mechanisms

The principle of "user pays" introduced early in the public sector reforms has been further developed.

Management of Policy-making

A significant feature of the restructuring of public service departments has been the separation of the policy advisory functions of departments from the operating functions and the establishment of small policy ministries. The aim of this separation of the policy and advisory from the administrative and operational functions has been to avoid a situation where policy advice is dominated by the operational agency. This separation has also been guided by the principle that fundamental services should be kept close to government while those that can be removed are structured into stand-alone agencies.

The new state sector framework and the reduction of input controls has led to marked changes in the role and functions of former "control" departments, in particular the Treasury and the State Services Commission.

The *Treasury* has traditionally been responsible for two main functions: economic policy advice and financial management. Ministers' needs for economic policy advice continue, but the nature of the financial management function has changed from administering a centralised cash accounting and reporting system, with an emphasis on compliance with input controls, to overseeing and further developing a decentralised financial management system based on accountability for performance.

The large centralised accounting function formerly provided by the Treasury has been transformed (as all departments now have their own accrual accounting systems) to a small group who prepare the consolidated financial statements and provide the remaining centralised elements of the system.

The recent financial management reform process has also impacted on the role of the budget management function within the Treasury. The Public Finance Act 1989 requires departments to provide vastly improved ex ante information on the goods and services (outputs) they will deliver and the financial performance they expect to achieve. Budget Estimates information has therefore increased in quantity and improved in quality. Appropriation is on an accruals basis, with the mode of appropriation recognising the different market conditions under which departments produce their outputs.

During 1989 the *State Services Commission* (SSC) underwent a major restructuring, with the aim of shedding functions which provided services to other departments. The focus for Commission services became ministers rather than a mixture of ministers and departments. The Commission has four core functions: top appointments and Senior Executive Service support; reviews of departmental and chief executive performance; policy advice on government machinery and structures; human resources policy, including development of standards of personnel administration, and negotiation of conditions of employment. An *amendment* to the State Sector Act in December 1989 replaced the State Services Commission (comprising up to four members) with two statutory officers: the State Services Commissioner and the Deputy State Services Commissioner.

Department of the Prime Minister and Cabinet

Also during 1989, the structure of the Prime Minister's Office and the Cabinet Office were reviewed with the objectives of: improving the co-ordination of the conduct of government business; and improving the quality of the advice available to the Prime Minister and the Government, particularly in the economic and social areas.

The review recommended combining the Cabinet Office and the advisory side of the Prime Minister's Office into a *single* Department of the Prime Minister and Cabinet. The main advantage of such an arrangement, it was stated, would be to have all professional advice and the co-ordination function under a single chief executive, which would make the complex co-ordinating task of the Prime Minister much easier.

The new Department is not to act as a separate source of detailed advice on all aspects of government. Rather, its role is to:

— provide the Prime Minister with views on whether departments, whose duty it is to provide the detailed advice, are in fact doing so to the required standard;

— test that advice to ensure that it addresses all the appropriate issues and offers viable, sensible solutions; and

— insist on adequate co-ordination and co-operation in cases where issues cross departmental boundaries (as virtually all major issues do).

Performance, Accountability and Control

In addition to improving efficiency, a focus of the recent public sector reforms has been to clarify and sharpen accountability. Under the provisions of the State Sector Act, chief executives are directly responsible to the minister for the efficient management of the department. Senior executives of departments are appointed on limited, performance-based contracts, and ranges of rates for other employees (including increases based on performance rather than incremental steps) have been introduced. The State Services Commission has a role in reviewing the performance of chief executives (annually) and of departments (every 3-4 years).

At 1 January 1991, all of the current 46 core public sector entities had moved to the new financial management system. In order to do so, their outputs had been adequately specified and agreed between ministers, they were operating full accrual accounting and cash management systems, and were able to provide external financial reports within the new formats.

Implementation in all departments of a charge for capital employed and the payment of interest on departmental cash balances is required by 1 July 1991. The capital charge recognises the cost of the capital the Crown invests in departments and allows the full cost of producing outputs to be assessed. The capital charge encourages the efficient use of fixed assets while payment of interest on departmental cash balances acts as an incentive for efficient management of working capital.

The new set of reporting requirements for departments and the Crown will enable the financial position of the Crown and its performance during the year to be much more transparent than has been the case in the past. The first set of accrual financial statements of the departments of the Crown will be those for the half year ended 31 December 1991. From 1 July 1992, the reports of all the entities owned by the Crown will be combined in its financial statements.

The *Audit Office* continues to independently audit and report on the operations of all state sector organisations. Under the provisions of the Public Finance Act, the Audit Office must issue an audit opinion on annual and half-yearly financial statements, which now include statements of service performance. The Audit Office reports to Parliament rather than to the executive and hence has a different focus from other review agencies.

Future Directions

The description above is the situation as it existed up to the end of 1990. However, following a change of Government as a result of the General Election held in October 1990, some changes in policy direction and in the management of the process have been indicated, e.g. amendments to the State Sector Act in the area of chief executive appointments.

Some changes will flow from a Bill, introduced into the House of Representatives in December 1990 (and now awaiting the Royal Assent), which significantly reduces the amount of legislative regulation of the labour market. Changes proposed in the Bill include voluntary unionism, removal of compulsory coverage of national awards and the consequent ability to choose between collective or individual contracts, and a change in union involvement by allowing employees to negotiate on their own behalf or to appoint anyone, not necessarily a union, as a bargaining agent. At this stage, it is not clear how regulation of employment contracts through case law will develop.

The Bill brings about the same changes in the legislation governing the state services but with one major exception. That exception is the retention of the central role of the State Services Commissioner for negotiating all collective employment contracts. The present structures may be subject to change over time as employees begin to choose new, less centralised bargaining agents, and the bargaining arrangements may adapt in response to that.

NORWAY

Management of Policy-making

In November 1990, a new social-democratic government came into office. This followed the resignation of the previous centre-conservative government after one year in office.

Much importance is still attached to increasing the *efficiency and effectiveness* of central government. In connection with the last two changes of government, the ministerial structure has also been rearranged to a certain extent. Among the changes is the establishment of the Ministry of Labour and Government Administration. One of the purposes of this particular rearrangement was to simplify the policy connection between labour policy and public management policy.

The Labour Party emphasises more than the non-socialist parties the importance and value of a large public sector. This will imply the need of a well-run administration. It is assumed that the new Labour Government will make no major alterations in the extent of public sector. This does not exclude the question of the relationship between the public and private sectors from the agenda, but there will be no programme for large-scale privatisation.

The contents of the *Modernisation Programme* from 1987 are still the basis for modernisation of the public sector. This programme is now being continued in different parts of the administration.

The main goals are: strengthening political guidance and overall policy formulation; increasing agencies' autonomy in running day-to-day operations; emphasising goal achievement; improving the management of the public sector and the working conditions and opportunities for development of government employees.

Three main projects are described below. They were all started by the present or by the previous Government.

The Organisation of State-owned Enterprises

Today there are several different types of state-run commercial or semi-commercial activity which are channelled through different types of organisation, ranging from public enterprises, which are part of the state, to state-owned stock companies. Public enterprises have been common where state control was needed or wanted, and where private commercial activity was no option. This type of organisation has made the necessary amount of governmental instruction and control possible.

A committee has been appointed and given the task of developing a new and better *organisational model* for state-owned enterprises (not stock companies). The aim is a law which will give the companies a more unambiguous relationship both to public enterprises and to state-owned stock companies. The intention is to find the proper balance between scope and type of strategic political management and public control, and managerial flexibility under market conditions. In addition, the committee is also expected to consider different aspects of the responsibility of the state as an owner. The next step will be to consider which of the existing public enterprises should be reorganised into the new model.

Another committee has been appointed to propose guidelines for the use of *boards* of public agencies, enterprises, companies and foundations. The reduction of the number of public boards, and the assignment of a more central position in management to the remaining boards, are issues to be discussed. Another important question is how these different kinds of board should be working, and what the limits of their responsibility ought to be.

Management of Regulatory Review and Reform

In Norway, like in most western societies, there is a consensus that laws ought to be simplified. Work on this is taking place in different areas.

In 1989, the Government appointed a committee with the purpose of examining the structure of the laws. In going through the existing laws, the committee was expected to bring forward proposals suggesting which laws were necessary and which were not, which laws could be abolished, and which laws might be combined with other existing laws. The result of the first report was that 321 laws were abolished by Parliament. This means that the number of laws was reduced by about one-third (from a total of about 1 000). The next report will be finalised during 1991. In addition, the committee has been given the task of proposing how different provisions and regulations could be better structured.

In 1990, the Government appointed another committee which will consider the possibilities of simplifying and modifying laws regulating trade and industry in order to make it easier to establish oneself in business.

A project aiming to make proposals on how to simplify regulation concerning public officials will also be commenced in 1991.

Administrative Development: the "OMEGA" Project

The OMEGA project is a joint venture between the Ministry of Labour and Government Administration and a major private Norwegian data company. The aim of the project is to develop and produce task flow systems for the 1990s, primarily directed towards public administration.

The main activities are to: increase the know-how and awareness of participants; develop supplier-independent user specifications; and develop prototypes of products at the data company to be the basis for further commercial products.

The project is expected to bring forward general user specifications for task flow systems. This basis will be further developed by Statskonsult (Directorate of Public Management) in co-operation with the Ministry of Labour and Government Administration. The first version of this system will be published in 1991.

PORTUGAL

Improving the Delivery of Public Services

The Government established a *"National Day for Debureaucratisation"* on 25 October 1990, to be celebrated every last Tuesday of October. The aim is to raise awareness, mobilise resources and promote initiatives to facilitate the formalities requested of the public and to simplify administrative procedures.

A protocol between the Secretary of State for Administrative Modernisation and the Secretary of State for Science and Technology was signed with the aim of providing financial support to an advance training programme in public management, to be held in national and foreign institutions. Junior graduates in management and administration as well as managers and high-level technicians will have access, through this programme, to research subsidies and to scholarships for masters degrees, PhDs and other training programmes in public management. This protocol was one of the initiatives to celebrate the first National Day for Debureaucratisation.

Ten *Consumers' Information Municipal Centres* have been established, through protocols between the National Institute for Consumers' Defense and ten municipalities, as an extension of work in settling disagreements between the administration and its clients.

The *Project Team for Debureaucratisation* of the Secretary of State for Local Administration has collaborated with ten municipalities with the aim of simplifying the procedures for municipal users within the context of the work of the Commission for Enterprise/Administration Relationships. The Commission, in cooperation with industrial associations for public works, textiles, clothing, shoes and food processing, is making an inventory of bureaucratic difficulties in these sectors with the objective of implementing debureaucratisation measures.

A new *Code of Administrative Procedures* was approved by the Government as part of the National Debureaucratisation Day initiative. This code provides the legal framework for the relationship between the administration and citizens. It defines reciprocal rights and duties. This new law enhances the policy of administrative modernisation, creating conditions to attain the objectives of accessibility to the public, debureaucratisation, transparency and personalisation of services, as well as simplifying the relationship between citizens and the administration.

Market-type Mechanisms

Following the Constitutional amendment approved in July 1989, and in accordance with Law No. 11/90 of 5 April 1990 (Lei Quadro das Privatizações), the Government started a vast *reprivatisation* programme covering banks, insurance companies, and beer enterprises.

The new Law establishes as reprivatisation aims, among others, the re-enforcement of the capacity of national enterprises and the reduction of state influence in the Portuguese economy. The Law also establishes reprivatisation procedures and stipulates rules concerning shares acquisition or subscription by the companies' workers, small subscribers and emigrants. The Law specifies the purposes of the revenues obtained from the reprivatisations, i.e. paying off the national public debts and debts of the public enterprises, as well as new investments and compensating the previous owners.

In 1990, the following Portuguese institutions were reprivatised: Unicer (51 per cent), Totta & Açores Bank (31 per cent), Transinsular (51 per cent), Tranquilidade (51 per cent), Centralcer (100 per cent), and Portugues do Atlantico Bank (33 per cent).

The Government intends to continue its own reprivatisation programme during 1991 and it is foreseen that this will cover insurance enterprises, banks, and cement companies.

Introduction and Use of Information Technology

The Institute of Informatics, together with the Presidency of the Council of Ministers and the Secretariat for Administrative Modernisation, are preparing a *data bank of citizens' information (INFOCID)*. The data bank will contain information on users' (citizens') duties, procedures and rights, how to address the administration, and what services are available from the administration. It is fed by the various ministries and diffused to the public by videotext through the public network. This project has received official recognition with the establishment of a high-level committee headed by the Secretary of State for Administrative Modernisation, due to submit recommendations to the Government at the end of 1991.

In the area of public finance, the main achievement has been the establishment of a centralised *budget information system* oriented toward the end user. The emphasis on software development concerning budget management and control is, however, now shifting towards decentralisation. This is required to support a major overhaul of procedures. The Budget Department will implement a reform in 1991 which will give greater autonomy to individual administration agencies.

In 1990, large-scale nation-wide automatic data processing operations for the new *income and property taxes* were possible for the first time. These procedures, largely based on taxpayer identification by means of a specific numeric code, implied major efforts both in software development — still in progress for the later stages — and automatic processing. The property data base which is gradually being assembled promises to provide for diverse applications.

A *legislation data base project (INFOJUR)* has been the subject of intensive methodological development for the last two or three years. It is now progressing through the contributions of several administration departments in the sectoral bases under their responsibility. In addition, there has been some refinement of software, concentrating on the development of friendly interfaces both for input and output.

The implementation of the *government office network project (RING)* is proceeding with infrastructure layout at three pilot ministries. Regarding software, the project has provided a new impetus for the Portuguese office automation system ELENIX and the implementation of several enhancements to that system.

The Ministry of Industry is implementing a data communications network conforming to the X25 norm which is to connect the three main cities in continental Portugal with a gateway to the public data network TELEPAC. It is intended to support the circulation of the Ministry's management information, including the control of financial support funds for the European Communities, and also to provide improvements to the use of IT resources (a matter which poses problems of integration).

The research/university sector has been quite actively using the available facilities prompted by European Research Programmes such as Race, Eureka, and Esprit. The FCCN network for the scientific community set up in 1989 has become permanently established.

There has been a *reorganisation of the communications sector* (still mostly state-owned), thus preparing the implementation of the recommendations of the Green Paper of the Commission of the European Communities. A recently created regulatory body, the Instituto de Comunicações de Portugal, is reaching fully operational status. In addition, a new enterprise, Telecom Portugal, was created, thus distinguishing the telecommunications arm of state operations from its other areas (e.g. post).

Human resources is a great concern in IT management, as elsewhere. New legislation concerning civil service careers and pay grades in the area of IT has been prepared, with involvement by the trade unions. It is due to be published before the end of 1990.

Parliament has approved a new law concerning IT data security and the protection of individuals' rights relative to IT-stored information.

SPAIN

Throughout the review period the Ministry of Public Administration (MPA), the department responsible for the civil service and organisational aspects of the central administration, was pushing ahead with the implementation of an ambitious *modernisation plan* for public service management. It covers organisational aspects as well as management procedures and human resources management.

Overall Plan of the Modernisation Process

Examination of the procedures and strategies developed by OECD Member countries, and in particular European Community countries, together with an analysis of the biggest problems in the Spanish administration, enabled the MPA to produce a document entitled *Reflections on the Modernisation of the Public Administration* at the end of 1988 (hereafter referred to as the document).

The principal conclusions of this document share the approach of the publication of the Technical Co-operation Committee, *Administration as Service: The Public as Client* (OECD, Paris, 1987). The process of modernisation has to be based on a new public service culture that regards citizens as "clients".

The "modernisation philosophy" that underlies the document is the idea of gradual, progressive transformation born from within, achieved through the application of the new culture, as opposed to the traditional concept of reform understood as a law or series of laws intended once and for all to establish a new organisational and functional model for the administrative apparatus. The new approach is based on the fact that the administration has to constantly adapt to new social demands, though at certain times this process has to be more intensive or more sustained.

Organisational Criteria

Analysis of the organisational model prevailing in the central administration reveals a number of dysfunctional elements. Some factors that contribute to this situation are:

— Ministerial departments are not structured for complete and clearly defined areas of operation, which leads to problems of shared or overlapping responsibility for the decisions affecting each area.

— Considering the department as an "administrative unit" is inappropriate from the standpoint of service management. There is no distinction between the ministerial portfolio, the unit for political decision, and the department as a management body.

The document proposes that as a first step towards rationalisation, each major functional area should be a basic organisational unit, what we shall call the *administrative module*. To this end, the functional area for which a module is responsible should be one that covers all the state responsibilities for a homogeneous branch of activity, thus creating functional unity and allowing differentiated management to suit the case.

The basic characteristics required of a module to facilitate effective management are that:

— it is a *self-sufficient structure* for the fulfilment of the assigned tasks, endowed with all the necessary resources including common services;

— it has the capacity to introduce *decentralised management* responsible for the results of its activity and endowed with the specific material and instrumental tools required for developing its programmes, formal ad hoc controls being replaced by performance appraisal;

— its *internal organisation* has the flexibility necessary for the nature of its activities and makes it possible for bodies of different types and different legal status (for example, centralised services and autonomous bodies) to fit in wherever the connection between the activities of different bodies calls for joint overall management.

Functional Aspects and Procedures

The document proposes the progressive incorporation of an integrated system of *management by objectives* which will enable the administration to progress towards the desired levels of effectiveness and efficiency. This system, conceived as a basic philosophy for public service action, can be generally applicable throughout the whole of the administration, though not all the management techniques associated with it will be applicable in all departments. Here the document proposes flexible adaptation of the system to fit the characteristics of each organisation and introduction in stages, starting with centres which provide services directly to the public where it is easier to set objectives, allocate resources, establish indicators and evaluate results.

In the field of budgeting, it is considered necessary to place more emphasis on the effective allocation of public resources through programme budgeting, taking account in each case of determinants for the application of this technique in the administration. For this it is proposed to progressively change the budgeting structure to better suit the action programmes and to associate the manager more closely with the process of drawing up budgets, with the aim of achieving the *effective integration of programmes and their budgets.* Here it would be useful to work towards the formulation of budget agreements with the managers as a possible way of linking them more closely with the attainment of the objectives set.

The *decentralisation of management* is not only one of the conceptual pillars of the document, but also a prerequisite for the essential functioning of the model. This decentralisation, which should place within the module all the decision-making responsibilities required for its autonomous operation, concerns on the one hand all powers over the material sector of activity in which the module operates, and on the other the management of the resources necessary to successfully carry out its specific activity.

Some of the proposals contained are: autonomy in budget implementation, working towards the elimination of prior external control (other than for specific exceptions) of the legality of expenditure records, which should become the responsibility of the module's own management; extension of the margin for budget modification in the field of approved programmes; autonomy for the design of the internal structure of the module in accordance with certain previously established general criteria; and more room for manoeuvre in human resources management in such fields as recruitment, pay, etc.

The decentralised management model set out requires a *new monitoring and control mechanism* to make it possible to take early corrective action and evaluate the results obtained in relation to the objectives set and the cost involved. The information system therefore plays a vital role, replacing the previous controls which it is proposed to abolish or reduce. This information system must be set up to take account of the new modular organisation. It has to be homogeneous in its basic aspects — the information transmitted to departments responsible for the whole of the administration — but at other levels the information required should be adapted according to the particular organisation of each module and the way in which relations between the responsible ministry and the module are established. In order to achieve this, it is necessary to take advantage of the possibilities offered by new information technologies.

In the same way, the control mechanisms are to be established at two distinct levels — apart from the final control exercised by the Accounts Tribunal — in a certain way comparable to the external and internal audits used in the private sector.

The first level corresponds to internal units located in all the modular structures. This should develop *management control* (organisation, procedures, etc.) and evaluation of the success of programmes.

The second level, developed by bodies of a horizontal nature for the whole of the state administration, must exercise the control required to ensure the overall equilibrium of the system, particularly important in a model where there is greater autonomy and decentralisation than before. This second level would therefore include *financial auditing,* controls to ensure *compliance* with criteria applicable throughout the administration (for example in the matter of staffing levels, pay, etc.), and specific *management audits.*

The most significant procedural proposals are, first, the implementation of a *checklist system* for the establishment of legal standards and for evaluation of the necessity, appropriateness and viability of normative proposals. Second, it is proposed to develop a *"prototype" administrative procedure* to serve as a compulsory model when introducing or modifying concrete procedures in each sector of activity. This would guarantee that, whatever the purpose of the procedure, the principles established by the prototype would be retained in all aspects concerning the subjective rights or legitimate interests of individuals.

Lastly, it is necessary to make the internal action mechanisms more efficient through the application of two basic principles: first, *reduced formalisation* of many internal action "processes" where the rights and interests of individuals are not involved, replacing procedural regulations incorporated in legal standards by technical procedure manuals; second, the general application in this field of *new information technologies,* replacing the handling of documents by computerised information and data storage systems.

The advantages offered in the field of information technologies are of two types: technical (making management more responsive and simple) and cultural (the use of the new technologies encourages a more dynamic approach to the performance of the tasks set).

Human Resource Criteria

The human resources management system is conceived in the document as an instrument in the service of the organisation, and of capital importance for the attainment of its objectives. From this standpoint, the proposed model exhibits the following general traits.

First, the present general principle of a single statutory regime, which has often forced groups of very different types into the same mould, should be replaced by a few much *more open general rules* making it possible to adjust the regime of the different groups to suit the tasks they have to perform and the type of organisation to which they belong. Obvious examples of these very different groups in Spain are, among others, teaching staff, health workers, postal staff, the armed forces, security people, etc.

Each of these groups requires "ad hoc" treatment that establishes the scope of the occupation, the career path, appropriate pay structures, system of entry, promotion, etc. A partial example of this line of work is given by the recent Decree on university teachers' pay, which is based on periodical appraisal of teaching and research activities.

Second, it is considered essential to give the administration the *necessary instruments for strategic human resources management.* The essential tool will be the *registers of posts* (Relaciones de Puestos de Trabajo, also discussed in the last section of this chapter), which when complete and improved will include the organisation of departments and organisations, job descriptions and the profile for each job with all the qualities required of its holder. This will allow an outline to be drawn up of the areas of activity or families of job that constitute the natural scope of the different career paths, and an adjustment to be made to the system of entry to the public administration according to the different categories and the planned manpower requirements.

An essential component in this area is the use of information technologies, which make it possible to centralise the complete and up-to-date information necessary for making strategic decisions and for the control of powers that are exercised in decentralised fashion by local managers.

The far-reaching *decentralisation of personnel management* is the third basic feature of the proposed model, in accordance with the document's general philosophy of making the manager responsible and allocating the specific resources required for attaining the objectives set for each organisation. The extent of this decentralisation will vary according to the type of staff (managerial or administrative, for example). In any event, within the general framework of standards and criteria established centrally, managers will tend to have more opportunity to select their own staff, at least on the internal market, and to fix the pay for the job within previously defined limits.

The document also stresses the vital importance of *training* for the renewal of the administration. This implies a major change in the present disinterested attitude both on the part of the administration and of its staff. The document suggests that priority be given to ongoing training to update the skills required for performing the job and encouraging the decentralised implementation of training plans, without any prejudice to the important role that will still be played by the central schools.

Implementation Strategy: Diffusion and In-depth Study of Proposals

Modular organisation should fit in with a strategy based on flexibility and progressiveness. Unlike the traditional idea of reform, there is no attempt to establish any legal standard for the number and organisation of modules. It is thus a matter of working from within the present organisation in order to examine the real possibilities for change.

As from the second quarter of 1989, the MPA document has been circulated and discussed with the other ministerial departments and sectors concerned, resulting in the incorporation of certain suggestions and the modification of certain aspects of the first draft. Up to now there have been presentations and debates of a global nature within the central administration with:

— high political authorities, including all the Secretaries of State, Under-Secretaries and Secretaries-General;

— Directors General, who are technical and political authorities with direct responsibility for the substantive units of the central administration;

— Subdirectors General, who constitute the highest technical management level. In view of the number of persons involved (some 1 500), these meetings will be continuing until the end of the first quarter of 1991.

To ensure diffusion in other fields, and in addition to the above, there were meetings during 1989 and 1990 to present and discuss the proposals with:

— parliamentarians of the Public Administration Committee of the Congress of Deputies;

— representatives of the public administration unions;

— university teachers from the faculties of law, economics, political science and sociology;

— journalists specialising in public administration matters;

— politicians and senior civil servants from other territorial administrations (Autonomous Communities and municipalities) who expressed to the MPA their interest in the modernisation proposals even though they were originally intended for the central administration only.

With regard to the working groups and meetings to study concrete aspects of the document, the major actions have been:

— *A survey of public managers' evaluation of the modernisation proposals.* 313 public managers (Directors General and Subdirectors General), who were selected by the MPA using sampling techniques, were sent a questionnaire containing the diagnosis of the existing situation and the modernisation proposals, grouped into six areas: general diagnosis, human resources, procedures, programming and budgeting, control and monitoring, information and its processing. The greatest consensus concerning strategies for change was found on the following aspects: the need to train public managers; reform of the mechanisms for budgeting and controlling expenditure; application of the new information technologies; increased autonomy for public managers through the decentralisation of powers.

— The setting up of an interministerial *Committee of Experts on Human Resources Management (CORHAP).* This Committee worked throughout 1989 to formulate proposals for human resources management. The experts of the central administration kept in touch with managers in big public and private enterprises and designed the bases of a computerised management model and the structure, functions and job profiles for the human resources units, according to the size of the organisation concerned.

— Creation of a *working group to study the remaining common services.* This MPA working group, together with five ministerial departments selected as a sample, examined the existing organisation and problems of the different common services (budget management, legal advice, management of material resources, etc.) and formulated a series of recommendations for action on organisation and procedures (elimination of legal control procedures, new information mechanisms, monitoring and evaluation of results, etc.). These recommendations are the subject of the "micro" implementation actions discussed below.

— Empowering of the *Higher Information Processing Council* to promote various projects, in the short and medium terms, connected with new information technologies and in particular the role of IT in the modernisation process. Some significant work during 1989 and 1990 includes:

  i) Production of an inventory of computer resources in the central administration and establishment of mechanisms to produce an annual update.

ii) The PRISMA project, which consists of the identification of opportunities for modernising the central administration through the use of information technologies and systems. To date 40 projects of an interministerial nature have been pre-selected, on the basis of the advantages they offer in view of the integration of Spain into the Europe of 1993, the degree of innovation they introduce into services, qualitative improvements, cost reductions, etc. The projects finally selected will have priority when the time comes to make investments in this field.

iii) Proposal to create IT staff units in the central administration to alleviate the shortage in the civil service. The creation of such units was realised through the General Central Budget Law of 1990, and the process of integrating existing computer staff and the selection of new staff will begin shortly.

iv) Creation of the Centre for Computer Studies (CREI), multiplying the number of specialist courses available. There is a plan for this Centre to shortly be converted into an autonomous body with its own management and separate legal status.

v) Production of technical guides for public managers, to facilitate the procedures for contracting computer equipment and services, and simplification of the authorisation procedures for the acquisition of such goods and services on the part of the ministries concerned (Ministry of Economics and Finance, and Ministry of Public Administration).

vi) Holding of the first one-day seminars on information technologies in the central administration, to diffuse knowledge of the advances made in this field and stimulate the application of these technologies in the different public services.

Implementation Strategy: Pilot Modernisation Experiments (macro action)

This consists in implementing global changes negotiated with organisations that voluntarily accept to apply the modernisation principles and that have been selected by the MPA.

The first aim of these pilot schemes is to *promote improvements in the management* of the entities selected, introducing new action procedures and giving managers more autonomy and new control mechanisms. Second, the pilot schemes are intended to *evaluate the results* of the concrete implementation of the principles contained in the document, so that any necessary corrections can be made before proposing that they should be generally applied.

Third, they are intended to *stimulate change in the culture* of the different organisations, for which purpose proposals for improvement in external and internal management are discussed with the entities concerned, and their specific problems are examined. This results in an *"agreement-programme"* containing the obligations assumed by the participants in the pilot scheme, i.e. on the part of the MPA (to solve the problems identified and facilitate management improvements), the ministry to which the entity belongs (to give it greater autonomy), and the selected entity itself (commitment to make improvements, with evaluation indicators).

A) *Involving changes in legal status*

In some cases, the changes in organisation and functioning have made it necessary to alter the legal status of the entity. This has been done through the General Budget Laws of 1990 and 1991. Specifically, these changes affect the following bodies.

Spanish Tourism Institute

This is a module (according to the criteria described when dealing with the principles of organisation) responsible for managing tourism policy in accordance with the directives of the central administration. It has been created as an autonomous commercial entity with a large degree of freedom in the management of its budget and its human resources, bringing together all the central organs of Spanish tourism policy in order to ensure unity of action based on a system of management by objectives. This module is responsible for the state enterprise that manages the government-run tourist hotels (Paradores) and the Official School of Tourism, basic instruments to promote a specific positive image of the quality of Spanish tourism and to train future professionals in this field of great importance to the Spanish economy.

State Tax Agency

The General Secretariat for Finance is part of the central administration and is subject to the traditional rules of organisation and functioning. It has a staff of some 25 000 people and manages a budget of Ptas 78 billion. The 1991 Budget Law created the State Tax Agency as a public entity with considerable management autonomy. This aimed to: ensure that the Agency manages state taxes more effectively, improve services to taxpayers, make it possible to provide services to other territorial entities, provide incentives to promote the achievement of the tax revenue objectives.

The principal innovations in this modernisation strategy are that:

 i)   The Agency is responsible for its own internal organisation, personnel and budget;

 ii) Part of the Agency's income depends on the extent to which the tax revenue objectives set for each fiscal year are achieved;

 iii) New systems of external control are being established to make it possible to evaluate the Agency's effectiveness, without adding any management difficulties. In the same way more responsive types of action are being designed to help achieve its objectives (contracting, economic management, personnel management, etc.);

 iv) The MPA is assuming responsibility for establishing the general criteria for organisation and personnel, and providing advice to the Agency while the project is being implemented.

"Post and Telegraph Agency" (PTT)

The General PTT Directorate is part of the central administration. This causes serious management problems. The PTT has a staff of some 67 000 people and manages a budget of Ptas 123 billion. The 1991 Budget Law created an autonomous commercial body with a "tailor-made" field of operation in line with its special nature. This change is aimed to: orient the body towards a management style similar to that of PTTs in other EEC countries, promote competition with the private sector in service quality, and make it self-financing through the elimination of exemptions from postal charges within three years.

The principal innovations of this transformation are:

 i)   A more responsive management framework for its services, by establishing a new regime for managing its own property and easing of the conditions governing contracting;

 ii) Great autonomy in the management of its own internal organisation, property and personnel;

 iii) New system of economic management and accounting along private enterprise lines.

B)   *With no change in legal status*

In other cases the introduction of modernisation measures has not required any change in the legal status of the pilot body (at least not in the first phase). The *Higher Sports Council* and the *National Meteorological Institute* are in this situation. The main innovations in their management included in the corresponding "agreement-programme" are:

— Formulation and implementation of a system of management by objectives;

— Implementation of a staff performance appraisal system (applied to senior staff in the first phase);

— Setting of certain performance incentive criteria through a productivity fund associated with the attainment of objectives;

— A greater degree of autonomy in managing their own personnel with delegated powers to modify the register of posts;

— Decentralisation of certain powers in the field of budget management;

— Introduction of a computerised human resources management system;

— Design of a series of staff training courses in these bodies, adapted to the specific needs of their activities;

— Examination of the main problems existing in their internal management procedures and drafting of manuals to simplify procedures and make management more responsive, etc.

Implementation Strategy: Modernisation Activities in Specific Areas (micro action)

Among the different types of sectoral action considered to be the simplest to introduce and to have the greatest chance of producing results in the short term are the following.

Introduction of the *projects involving new information technologies* referred to above. Stimulating the efficient use of information technologies is at present one of the major activities of the MPA, covering various fields of application: information for the client (answers to all questions at the same desk), development of projects that facilitate the management of services, establishment of new systems that permit communication between ministerial departments, etc.

The years 1989 and 1990 saw the consolidation of the system of evaluation and control of services known as *"Service Operation Inspections"*. These aim to identify the problems in different areas of administrative action and draw up alternative solutions. Attempts to spread the use of this methodology and its results have been essentially through two channels: *a)* the publication and circulation of a document entitled "Service Operation Inspections", which has been published in Spanish, French and English; and *b)* the conclusion of co-operation agreements with other public administrations. Three such agreements have been concluded to date: with Catalunya, the Principality of Asturias and Barcelona Council.

As part of the policy of modernising and rationalising the public administration, two projects are being developed simultaneously with the aim of defining instruments to permit the evaluation of the functioning of the administration as a public service provider. These projects are: *a)* establishment of *indicators* to measure improvements in administrative action; *b)* identification of *problem areas* in the functioning of the administration. The work involved is ex-post comparative and dynamic evaluation, the findings being addressed to those in charge of the administration concerned.

The new concept of administration as service implies the need to democratise administrative language so as to make it comprehensible to the citizen. In order to modernise and simplify the language used by the administration, the *"Administrative Language Style Manual"* was published in 1990. It is aimed at public servants and attempts to provide concrete answers to concrete questions that arise when drafting administrative documents to be used by the public. It is also intended to encourage thought about the use of language and its applications in administrative communications and documents, with the aim of developing an administrative language that is clear, concise and suited to the requirements of modern and effective management.

In order to improve the quality, quantity and co-ordination of the information intended for the citizen, an *"integral plan for information for the citizen"* has been drawn up. Guidelines for the implementation of this plan have been collected into what is known as the "Project for the unified management of administrative information" (Proyecto Guia), which covers all public functions and services and sets out the steps to be followed by the citizen in his dealings with government agencies. This project involves the entire state administration.

As regards the introduction of new *budgeting, expenditure and control techniques* for such action, the Ministry of Economics and Finance has established certain mechanisms to simplify the procedures for prior control of the legality of expenditure. This type of control has also been replaced for financing the commercial activities of certain autonomous organisations. However, the generalisation of this type of measure — of particular importance — needs to be carefully studied and here what is learned from the pilot projects will be extremely useful.

Within this broad spectrum of proposals, the specific responsibility of the MPA covers, as has been said, those concerned with human resources and information technologies, together with the more general task of promoting the best type of organisation for the different services according to the nature of the tasks and functions of each. The importance of human resources in any organisation — and in particular in public organisations, where the great majority of civil servants spend their whole working life in the administration — has meant that this subject has been studied in considerable depth, and the last section of this chapter is devoted to it.

Innovatory Measures in the Field of Human Resources in the Spanish Administration

Throughout 1989 and 1990, there were many actions designed to ensure that the administration was staffed with the necessary number of people with the right skills to handle the challenge of modernisation and gradually incorporate the mechanisms essential for truly forward-looking human resources management.

Instrument for forward-looking human resources management

Human resources planning means that each organisation or management centre has to rationalise and formalise the structure of its units, and define the characteristics of each job category and the conditions for filling them.

In the past two years virtually all ministries and the organisations under their control have been given *registers of posts* (Relaciones de Puestos de Trabajo) containing job descriptions and profiles. The registers are instruments of great assistance to forward-looking management, making it possible among other things to check that the type of organisation is still suited to the tasks, to identify training needs, and to define promotion plans and career paths.

A *resolute decentralisation policy* has been introduced to give managers more autonomy in human resources management. Royal Decree 1084/90 of 31 August 1990 transferred to departments the greater part of the powers of the Directorate General of Public Administration over personnel management, leaving that Directorate with only certain major decision-making responsibilities such as handling the annual public service recruitment procedures.

This initiative is soon to be complemented by further decentralisation of the management of the registers of posts so that departments, within the framework of directives from the MPA, can decide on such matters as the creation, modification and elimination of posts, alteration of job content, and, within limits, remuneration.

Since the very beginning of the process of transforming human resources management in the Spanish administration, it has been recognised that it must be fully *supported by information technology*. There has therefore been complete computerisation of the human resources field, in order to support decentralisation and at the same time have all the information centrally available to the MPA as the authority responsible for defining overall manpower policies and strategies.

The *Central Staff Registry*, coming under the MPA, has developed the central and decentralised information technology infrastructures (with branches of the Registry in ministries, organisations and regional governments) and created various databases, notably staff records, registers of posts and legislation relating to human resources.

As a result, the MPA now has complete, highly reliable and constantly updated information about the entire staff of the central administration: personal data, career data, job held and its characteristics. In addition, the Registry has oriented its activity towards support for the different personnel units by offering a broad range of services with the aim of encouraging the complete computerisation of human resources management in all departments.

At present, through the branches of the Registry, the departments, organisations and regional governments have decentralised personnel management databases, in addition to being connected to the Registry's central database. Furthermore, various other computer applications have been introduced to support aspects of management such as internal staff selection and the storage of records on optical disk.

Objective of recruiting the personnel required by the administration

The Spanish administration has suffered in recent years from a significant fall in the number of candidates for Group A jobs (senior established staff) in the civil service. In view of this situation, the causes have been analysed and an initial revision is being made of certain *selection procedures* with the aim of achieving a better match between the skills required and the characteristics of entry-level jobs in the administration, together with more *flexibility* in recruitment dates.

The possibility is also being studied of gradually introducing more far-reaching changes in selection procedures, with the aim of reducing the relative weight of formal knowledge and giving more emphasis to candidates' aptitudes and new evaluation techniques (tests, interviews, simulation exercises, etc.). In connection with this, the importance is stressed of the *creation in 1990 of IT units in the central administration* with senior, middle level and junior level staff, respectively Principal of Information Technologies and Systems, Manager of Systems and Data Processing, and Data Processing Technical Assistants.

The creation of these units is intended to eliminate the shortage of IT professionals, increase the weight of IT services through professionalisation, attract new staff, bring in experienced professionals, and eliminate the present high mobility. The fact of being newly created units has facilitated the adoption of innovatory measures, namely: a new selection model based on psycho-technical and knowledge tests, English language and practical tests, and the definition of a career path organised according to personnel categories. The recruitment plans under the 1990 budget provide for the following additional IT posts: 150 senior, 250 middle and 400 junior level.

Improving staff efficiency and motivation

Training has developed considerably and has been re-oriented in two directions: first, *intensification* of training to meet the needs of the job; and second, greater *decentralisation* of training to the departments and organisations themselves. At the same time there has been a strengthening of the *National Institute for Public Administration* (INAP) as the major training centre for the central administration. Without prejudice to other training actions, this institute is to harmonise efforts in the formulation and development of directives. The INAP has drawn up a *management training plan* for 1991, giving priority to subjects of a directly applicable nature (organisation, planning, problem analysis, running meetings, etc.) and based on practical and interactive methods.

Performance appraisal systems have been developed and these will be introduced in a pilot organisation on an experimental basis in 1991. In order to ensure the proper functioning of these mechanisms, their implementation will be supported by prior definition of the objectives and duties of each person subject to evaluation, and the effects or consequences of the appraisal, including any rewards, will be clearly defined. This is intended to provide the manager with an instrument to support a decentralised personnel policy and at the same time to *improve staff motivation* through clarification of their promotion and career prospects.

A third measure, widely accepted by civil servants, has been the generalisation of the practice of filling job vacancies through *competitive examination among staff* of the administration itself, limiting the use of free appointment to Subdirector General posts and others with special responsibilities. This practice (i.e. according to candidates' merits, in particular specific merits suited to the characteristics of the post concerned) leads to greater stability in the posts thus filled.

The project aimed at transforming human resources management in the administration has not been inspired solely by the idea of improving it technically, directing the process from above, but has tried to actively *involve the staff* themselves, and in particular has taken the view that the *unions* should be more closely associated with the management of change in the personnel field. Law 7/90 significantly increased the powers of the unions as regards the working conditions of civil servants through the incorporation of new aspects into the *collective bargaining process*. Among them are the annual pay increases to be included in the central government budget, the determination of programmes and funds for promotion and training activities, and measures concerned with health at work.

Co-operation between Public Bodies

During 1989 and 1990, co-operation between the central government and the Autonomous Communities was developed according to engagements made in previous years. Two different instruments were used:

— *Agreements:* in each of the two years, 250 agreements were signed, the total resources allocated to these agreements being 94 and 193 thousand million pesetas respectively.
— *Bilateral or multilateral commissions:* approximately 250 have been created covering all sectors in which the Autonomous Communities have responsibilities.

In 1989, a special body was created within the Ministry of Public Administration with responsibility for periodic meetings between the minister and his regional counterparts with a view to dealing with the participation of the Autonomous Communities in matters relating to the European Community. The first agreements have already been concluded.

Supplementary Reference Material

Ministry of Public Administration (1990), "Reflexiones para la modernización de la Administración del Estado", Secretarío General Técnico and Instituto Nacional de Administración Pública (SGT-INAP), Madrid (Spanish text only).

Ministry of Public Administration (1988), "Service Operation Inspections", Madrid.

SWEDEN

The present guidelines for public sector renewal were presented by the Government in the Supplementary Budget Bill in the spring of 1989. Further developments are now in progress. The context and direction of the ongoing reforms of Swedish public management are set out in the summary of *The Swedish Budget 1990/91*, published by the Ministry of Finance (pages 184-186). Further details are given in Annex 2 of the Budget Bill for 1st July 1990 to 30 June 1991 and also in the Supplementary Budget Bill for 1st July 1991 to 30 June 1992, which is to be decided upon by Parliament in May 1991. The information below has been extracted from those three reports.

Developing the Public Sector

A vigorous build-up in the post-war period has made the public sector an essential component of Sweden's welfare society. The public sector in Sweden is very large compared with other countries and the distribution of welfare is higher and more uniform than in most other countries, due in large measure to the public service system. The extension of the public sector has also contributed significantly to equality between women and men.

Intensive efforts are being made to *develop and renew the public sector*. This is partly a consequence of new demands on this sector, some of which have to do with unsatisfied needs and queues, for instance in child care and care of the elderly. (A growing proportion of very old people will add to the demand for medical care, etc.). There is also a growing demand for *good quality, better access* and *variety*, for instance in medical care and education. There are still instances of schools and hospitals that differ markedly in quality. There are also differences and injustices that must be tackled in the provision of social care and education.

There are very limited possibilities, however, of providing additional resources for the public sector. This makes it essential, and a challenge, to *use existing resources* to greater effect. Priorities should be adjusted so as to provide room for urgent new needs. Efforts should be made to raise the productivity and efficiency of public activities.

In some cases it may be appropriate to alter the direction and organisation of these activities. *Decentralisation* and the *delegation of responsibility* should be greater than at present. Those who manage and implement public activities should have more freedom to decide how the objectives are to be achieved. These principles are being introduced in many areas, for instance the school system, public health and medical care, the penal administration, and care of the elderly.

— For the *school system,* the intention is that the Government and Parliament are to set out the objectives, while municipalities are to be generally responsible for running the system. Besides being important for achieving the objectives, this general responsibility will allow available resources to be utilised more efficiently since responsibility and decision-making will be located at the operational level. The recent decision by Parliament to discontinue the central government regulation of school posts is a feature of this work.

— The structure of the *public health service* is being reviewed by the Association of County Councils in co-operation with representatives from the Ministry of Health and Social Affairs and the National Board of Health and Social Welfare. The review is to cover the responsibility for and financing of primary care as well as care at county and regional levels. Proposals to create a unique centre of responsibility for care for the elderly were presented in the course of 1990, covering medical care as well as traditional forms of care for the elderly.

More *follow-up* and *evaluation of results* should be undertaken. Cost and result statistics that are comparable throughout the country should be produced. Politicians must accept the consequences of evaluations to a greater extent and alter priorities in the allocation of resources.

A clearer distinction is needed between responsibility for production and responsibility for financing. A wider use of tendering and contracting can result in a more varied supply and greater freedom of choice.

The ongoing *re-organisation of the budget process* means that more attention is being paid to the results of public activities. With the specification of a desired direction and expected results for various central government activities, steering will be more concerned with results. The foundation for this is the more detailed assessment which every authority is to make of its entire field every third year. The detailed regulation of public activities can then be decreased. Reviews are in progress, or being planned, of the system for steering and following up the defence administration, the decision process for assistance to developing countries, the presentation of results from research and higher education, structural and organisational issues in the police administration, etc.

Development and renewal work are also in progress in other fields, for instance central government personnel policy, information technology, and efforts to improve co-ordination and collaboration across public activities. Developing the public sector and improving its efficiency are some of the main tasks of economic policy.

The Administrative Reform Programme

In an address to the Riksdag (Parliament) in October 1990, the Government announced a programme for readjusting and slimming down the national administration. That programme has been presented in full in the Supplementary Budget Bill. The savings to the national budget are estimated at approximately SKr 2 000 million.

The basics of the programme can be summed up in three words: *decentralisation, deregulation, internationalisation.* The programme will run for the three fiscal years 1991/92, 1992/93 and 1993/94. The programme aims to *transform the national administration* and reduce it by 10 per cent over a three-year period. Several of the points which the programme included have already been put before the Riksdag, in the 1991 Budget Bill, in the Growth Bill or in specific legislative proposals. A number of further measures are now proposed, for implementation during the next few fiscal years.

Some of the aims of the reform programme relate to local authorities and central-local relations. They are dealt with in the next section. For the central administration, the essential aims are listed below.

Better co-ordination in pursuit of common objectives

The *allocation of responsibilities* between different authorities should be made as clear as possible. Decisions on co-ordination should be guided above all by the desirability of bringing together public activities which share common objectives. In certain cases, two or more authorities should amalgamate to form a single new one.

Examples can be cited: STU (the Board for Technical Development), SIND (the Industrial Board) and the National Energy Administration are to be abolished and replaced by a new authority for entrepreneurial policy. A new central agricultural authority is to be set up. Proposals are being drafted for the establishment of a new public health institute which will take over and develop further the intersectoral public health policy work being done at present by several different authorities.

Demand and competition

For the enhancement of efficiency, public activities should include a greater element of *quasi-commercial operation.* This will mean, for example, developing producer-client relations and financing a larger proportion of services out of direct charges. As an example, national statistical production should be governed more by demand. It is also proposed that the real-estate logistical activities of the National Board for Public Building be transferred to a demand-controlled service authority.

Adapting the national administration to an open Europe

Parts of the national administration and its structure, organisation, planning and budgeting cycles, and competence will be affected by the process of European integration. *Internationalisation* may require measures to achieve greater economy in some fields and, in others, additional resources. The readjustment of the national administration is therefore to proceed in such a way that opportunities for reaping administrative benefits can be acted upon, at the same time as the integration process can be conducted in keeping with the Riksdag's intentions. During the spring of 1991 the Government will be initiating an enquiry to consider measures whereby Sweden's administration can be suitably equipped for its tasks in the future process of integration.

Personnel questions connected with structural changes

Necessary structural rationalisation measures in the national administration are made feasible by the fact that it has probably the most *comprehensive and advanced job security system* in the Swedish labour market. In cases where duties are transferred from a disbanded to a newly-formed authority, the Government will issue special ordinances making it possible for personnel whose previous duties were of an essentially similar kind to be offered employment with the new authority.

Development of the working methods of the Government and its Chancery

During the past few years the Government Chancery (the Ministries), in common with extensive areas of the national administration generally, has significantly renewed its activities in several different fields. The *personnel* strength of the Government Chancery, not including the Ministry for Foreign Affairs, has been reduced by 200 persons since 1982, which means around 10 per cent. This is partially thanks to extensive delegations to agencies and others. Special programmes for a more appropriate structure of competence, personnel supply, and personnel development have been decided on and are now in the process of implementation. The main thrust of the Government Chancery's activities should be shifted further towards making more *articulate demands* on public activities, *following up results* and ensuring that *steering systems* operate efficiently. The organisation and working routines of the Government Chancery are to be reviewed as part of the readjustment and reduction of the national administration.

Fewer and simpler rules

For several years, extensive work has been in progress to simplify the rules governing public activities. A report on this subject was given in Schedule 2, Division 5 of the Budget Bill. All resource-consuming regulatory systems must be *scrutinised* to investigate the possibilities of reappraisal and simplification. Several of the proposed administrative simplifications call for extensive alterations to the regulatory systems, for example: in the field of social insurance, a number of regulatory changes are imminent, such as the introduction of an employer's liability period for sickness allowance and reforms to bring about active rehabilitation; and the new foodstuffs policy implies the dismantling of internal market regulations.

Management of regulatory review and reform

The impact on regulatory review of computerised data bases has continued to *reduce the number* of laws and ordinances in force in Sweden. According to statistics presented in the 1991 Budget Bill, as of 1st December 1990 their number was the lowest for at least 20 years. Similarly, as a result of the guidelines established for issuing regulations, there has now been a reduction by more than half in the number of administrative rules issued by the 24 county administrative boards.

Strengthening the Local Authority Level

The transition to management by results implies new demands on the central authorities, with the creation of considerable scope for *delegation* to regional and local levels. For example: management and resource utilisation in the higher education sector are now under review; responsibility for the administration of personnel and finance within the courts of justice and the public prosecution authorities should be transferred from, respectively, the National Courts Administration and the Prosecutor-General to the regional or the local level.

A *freer hand* is being given to *municipalities* through the abolition of detailed national regulations, thus improving the ability of municipalities to adapt their activities to the demands of the public. For example: a new Education Board is to be introduced, which will be mainly concerned with development, follow-up and evaluation; the central activities of the National Board of Health and Welfare are to concentrate on follow-up and evaluation, and the board's supervisory functions are to be taken over by regional units for public health, medical care and dental welfare.

There are now four county councils and 35 municipalities participating in the *"Free Local Government Experiment"* which sets aside mandatory application of uniform national legislation and regulations affecting the structures, organisation and operation of local authorities.

The Government now wishes to give municipalities and county councils *wider powers of discretion,* so that their activities can be streamlined and adapted to local conditions. The Government also wishes to give elected representatives in municipalities and on county councils better opportunities for controlling and directing activities in accordance with the needs and preferences of the citizens.

The proposed new Local Government Act (1990/91:117) concludes a *comprehensive process of reform* which has been advancing, by various stages, since 1984. The present Local Government Act, although passed as recently as 1977, is already outmoded as a result of the rapid changes which occurred in local government during the 1980s.

Provisions of the proposed Act, which is to be decided upon by Parliament in May 1991, include the following:

— *Entitlement to compensation for loss of earnings:* Elected representatives will be entitled by law to reasonable compensation for the loss of earnings entailed by their local government duties. The municipal council will decide, according to local circumstances, on the compensatory system to be applied.

— *Procedures for the control, direction and auditing of activities:* More scope will be provided for the delegation of business, both by the municipal council to specialised committees and within the committees themselves (e.g. to employees). The rules are framed in such a way as not to impair opportunities for public insight and inspection. The municipal council will acquire new instruments for following up the goals and guidelines it has laid down and for evaluating the results achieved by municipal committees. The latter in turn will be better placed to direct the administrative authorities under them and to encourage personnel by giving them wider responsibilities and powers.

— *Free structure of committees:* Municipal and county councils will be at liberty to decide for themselves how their committees are to be organised. A special executive board with duties of a general nature will remain mandatory, but the other committees which are mandatory under existing legislation (e.g. the building committee and the environment and health protection committee) will in future be optional. The tasks defined in special enactments will also remain mandatory and will be unaffected by the deregulation of local government organisation. A special statutory provision will guarantee that no committee is entrusted with incompatible duties. For example, a municipal committee cannot both operate an environmentally hazardous facility and be responsible for enforcing compliance with environmental regulations.

— *More clearly defined powers of local government:* The powers of municipal and county councils are to be more clearly defined. Thus the proposed Act includes special rules on several of the basic principles of local government law, e.g. the localisation principle and the equality of status principle. The proposed Act also defines the limits of municipal competence in the enterprise sector.

— *New rules regarding municipal enterprises:* The present Local Government Act contains no rules on the activities of municipal or county council enterprises. Under the proposed new Act, the councils will have to ensure that municipal enterprises are subjected to certain conditions designed to guarantee municipal or county council control over their activities. The council will also have to adopt public domain provisions for the records of every such enterprise.

— *New forms of financial management:* Instead of the present statutory safeguards for capital assets, municipal and county councils will be required to run their activities on a sound economic basis. They will be required to administer their funds so as to meet the requirements of a good return on capital employed and of adequate security. Operating income must not normally be used to finance day-to-day activities. Municipal and county councils will also be required to supplement their annual budgets with three-year economic plans.

— *More importance attached to accounting and auditing:* The proposed new Act calls for "consolidated accounting". In other words, the annual report is also to include particulars of the finances of municipal enterprises. The annual report is to be kept open to public inspection, and the municipal council may decide to hold a meeting at which members of the general public will be allowed to ask questions about the annual report. The scope of auditing responsibility will be extended to also include individual elected representatives.

— *Dismissal of elected representatives:* Under a new power to be conferred by the proposed Act, members of the executive board or municipal committees can be relieved of their duties by the municipal council if they have been refused discharge from liability or if they have been convicted of serious criminal offences.

— *Possibility of more rapid post-election impact:* The current rule is for the executive board to take office on 1st January the year after election year. Under the proposed new Act, municipal and county councils wishing to do so may allow the executive board to take office earlier, which in practice will mean as from the council's first meeting after the election. The option of a more rapid post-election impact also applies to other municipal and county council committees.

Supplementary Reference Material

GUSTAFSSON, Agne (1988), *Local Government in Sweden,* The Swedish Institute, Uddevalla (Sweden).
Ministry of Finance (1990), *The Swedish Budget 1990/91:*
A Summary, Allmänna Förlaget, Stockholm.
Ministry of Finance (1991), *The Swedish Budget 1991/92:*
A Summary, Allmänna Förlaget, Stockholm.

SWITZERLAND

On 17 September 1990 the Federal Council sent a message to Parliament concerning the partial revision of the Act on the Organisation of the Administration (Secretaries of State, General Secretaries, delegation of powers). The General Secretariat has been given a wider mandate. A draft ordinance on working relations between General Secretaries and heads of information services in departments is currently being prepared.

A system for monitoring the administration has been set up. A parliamentary body for "control" of the administration was created by the parliamentary initiative of the Management Commissions of 12 February 1990 and the opinion of the Federal Council of 14 February 1990.

"Management Control" in the Federal Administration

Developed in Germany, "management control" is a known and proved method of work in the private sector, particularly in Germany, Austria and Switzerland, where it is mostly used for the judicious exploitation of accounting data. The question arose whether it could help the management of day-to-day work of the administration.

In 1989, the Federal Department of Finance (DFF) launched a study on management control to find out whether and to what extent it could in particular:

— support the management effort of departments so as to optimise their efficiency and effectiveness;
— facilitate the examination of DFF expenditure;
— clarify the objectives set by the legislature and determine to what extent they are achieved;
— gradually bring about better planning and better political and financial management.

Strategic and/or operational piloting

Contrary to what might be expected, the word "control" is used in the English sense of "adjust, direct, guide" rather than the French usage of "verification". Management control is a method of work which permits management to be monitored in an optimum way, so as to help those in charge to intervene in good time and as and when necessary. Management control involves the *systematic processing of information* whereby it is possible to bring together, receive in good time, present in summary form, and more particularly evaluate all information seen as essential for management.

To do this, management control concentrates on basic information concerning objectives pursued, priority tasks, available resources, working conditions, the results of management, the criteria enabling those results to be evaluated with respect to objectives, and their inter-relationships.

The diagram below shows the information to be monitored and possible intervention (adjustment) by the responsible bodies.

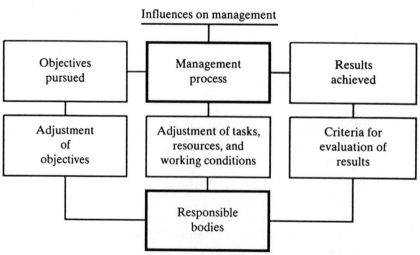

In principle, such a scheme seems self-evident. However, it appears that the objectives of administration are not always clear and that results are fairly rarely analysed. What is more, management control provides a systematic approach to, and a global view of, management which are otherwise often lacking.

Management control should make possible regular comparisons between what was planned and what is actually happening. To do this, management control divides the activity up into intermediate objectives so as to follow trends at various prescribed times and influence them as appropriate.

Management control also offers a philosophy of management leading to analysis which is *basic* (replying in particular to the questions: Are objectives pursued still adequate? Are methods and resources used to achieve these objectives the right ones?), *global* (allowing for internal factors and the environment in the broad sense) and *dynamic* (reflecting interactions and changes over time but clearly directed at the future).

Management control thus aims to permanently facilitate optimum strategic and operational decision-making at all echelons and consequently the achievement of the objectives set. The operative word is "facilitate" rather than "ensure" good decision-making, since management will continue to depend on the quality of those in charge and the influences bearing on them. Relations between official goals and what is actually done may sometimes be distorted to promote "federalist" economic or political interests (support for a canton or region). In such cases, management control makes it easier to understand the consequences.

Finally, it is important to stress that the outcome of management control is a living form of work organisation and not some immutable structure. Flows of information on management and assessment criteria must also be reconsidered at regular intervals to make sure that they were the right ones and that they remain valid in a constantly changing environment.

Lessons to be drawn from the first pilot projects

Of the four initial pilot projects, selected to give a representative cross-section of the activities of the federal administration, three are already being carried out. One was discontinued, as the expected results appeared to be far too limited.

The first important finding emerging from the pilot projects is that management control is a method which can be applied in numerous fields of administrative work.

So far as the utility of management control is concerned, this was examined from the standpoint of the four objectives to be achieved. The assessment is a tentative one based on the results of the conceptual stage and the first steps towards implementing the three projects.

Support the management effort of departments so as to optimise their efficiency and effectiveness

The projects were defined by the federal departments concerned, having regard to their needs and possibilities. Thus departments had to first clarify their task and secondly play an active part in the conception of the management control system.

It became apparent that, to set up an operational management control system, departments had to give detailed thought to their legal terms of reference and to how they managed their activities, and that this in itself produced ideas for appropriate innovations. Moreover, it is obvious that such a systematic and comprehensive approach to management can help optimise efficiency and effectiveness, starting with greater rigour in planning.

The use of this information system will also facilitate and speed up strategic and/or operational decisions by departments, since they will have a better understanding of their objectives, of the resulting choice of priorities and of the results to be expected from action undertaken.

Support the Federal Department of Finance in its examination of expenditure

Participation in management control projects has enabled the DFF to better understand individual areas of expenditure, which in itself makes the examination easier. Moreover, completion of management control projects will gradually bring a noticeable improvement in quality and in the relevance of information regularly supplied to the DFF on the fields in question.

Clarify the objectives set by the legislature and determine to what extent they are achieved

Since the definition and delineation of objectives is an essential condition for organising a system of management control, clarification, understanding and in some cases interpretation of the intentions of the legislature are necessary. Furthermore, by reason of quantitative and/or qualitative assessment criteria introduced, the results of management will be evaluated and regularly compared with the desired objectives. Having regard, in addition, to the analysis of changes occurring in the activity covered by management control and in its environment, the responsible bodies will thus have the necessary information to check the validity of these objectives or, where necessary, will be able to make modifications in consequence.

Gradually bring about better planning and better political and financial management

Management control is not only a method of work, it is also a philosophy of management as explained above. Moreover, management control, through its systematic approach, requires a very clear allocation of powers and, for this reason, means more autonomy for certain decisions as well as greater responsibility at various levels of the hierarchy. From this standpoint, management control will, as it becomes better known and understood by those in charge and executive staff, make it possible to improve their planning and management capabilities.

Consequences from the organisational standpoint

The introduction of management control is not difficult, but requires detailed analysis of a given area and active participation by managers and the staff concerned. Such work is not a normal function of departments and thus poses problems at the outset. The pilot projects have nevertheless shown that it is of particular interest for those concerned.

Furthermore, it is interesting to note that the introduction of management control does not as a rule require any additional staff, but does involve changes in the way existing staff work. In addition, resulting data processing requirements can, in many departments, be met by existing resources.

Follow-up to the project

On the basis of these initial results, the Federal Council decided in January 1991 to introduce management control on a large scale throughout the federal administration. A new series of pilot projects is also to be set up this year in order to get a better understanding of the limits and possibilities of this method of management and define the methodology more clearly.

Supplementary Reference Material

WITSCHI, A., EGLI, H. J., and TORIEL, E. (1990), "Controlling dans l'Administration fédérale: Phase 3: Concepts détaillés (Parties I et II)", Zurich (French and German text only).

WITSCHI, A., EGLI, H.J. (1990), "Controlling in der Bundesverwaltung: Phase 2: Prüfen der Machbarkeit", Zurich, (German text only).

TURKEY

Government programmes clearly state that the public administration should be reorganised towards a more responsive, efficient, effective and speedy administrative system in accordance with national interests, national goals, and economic and social developments. These objectives have been treated as outstanding issues, and the necessary amendments to existing legislation have been made and a number of new regulations have been enacted so as to ensure the responsiveness and effectiveness of public management bodies.

In Turkey, studies for *reducing the burden of bureaucracy* on relations between citizens and the administration and consequently the simplifying of administrative procedures have been continuing since 1984. Projects on public management improvement are being implemented by relevant administrative agencies within the framework of the following main principles:

— saving time and resources in administrative procedures;

— accepting personal declarations as legitimate in transactions between the public and the administration unless it is deemed necessary to require justification through appropriate documents;

— establishing a "one-stop shop" system;

— delegating authorities to lower hierarchical levels with the aim of effectiveness and efficiency in the public administration.

So far, the total number of *measures* including legislative and regulatory improvements has exceeded 500. Some specific projects which have been completed successfully in 1990 are listed below.

— Pension payments to retired persons, widows and orphans are now transferred directly to their bank accounts and the system of payment by cheque has been abolished. The beneficiaries have enjoyed the advantages of advanced technologies as has the national economy by encouraging bank savings.

— Time-consuming formalities for obtaining hunting licences have been simplified.

— Employment of temporary workers by public agencies and organisations has been accelerated.

— Auditing and control authority over payments to elderly and infirm Turkish citizens has been delegated from the Ministry of Customs and Finance to the Government Public Pension Office for Civil Servants, thereby speeding up operational response times.

— Ratification of medical certificates for imported medical equipment used by disabled persons has been delegated from the Ministry of Health to local health offices, thereby reducing completion time.

— Working procedures of the commission which grants pharmaceutical licences have been rescheduled to reduce delays.

— The custom duties charged on imported goods can now be paid at the customs office where the importation occurs rather than going to the nearest city with a tax office.

— Visas may now be issued to foreign tourists by tourist companies, thus reducing crowds at frontier customs.

— Compulsory "triptic" procedures for Turkish citizens coming from foreign countries with their own vehicles have been abolished, and filling out the "entrance form of vehicles" has been deemed as sufficient. In consequence, temporary import procedures have been simplified and unified.

— Medical services received by members of BAG-KUR (Social Security Agency for small and medium-scale enterprise owners) have been broadened.

— The civil Registration Law has been amended, resulting in improvements and simplifications regarding the fines for failing to promptly register changes in civil status.

— Public service activities for sailors who sail in Turkish Territorial Waters gained effectiveness by the dissemination of frequent information about meteorological forecasts through mass media.

— Formalities for lighthouse and rescue payment procedures for Turkish yachts and scientific vessels which are up to 100 NRT (national registered tonnage) and sailing in Turkish Territorial Waters have been abolished. All other formalities stipulated for vessels up to 300 NRT have been minimised and bureaucratic simplification has been ensured by introducing an annual payment system.
— The obligation for the health card declaration and registration of all yachts which sail in Turkish Territorial Waters has been abolished.
— The obligation for yachts sailing between Turkish ports without leaving Turkish borders to possess and to declare a customs inventory list has been abolished.

Management of Human Resources

Employment in ministries and public agencies is being scrutinised and studies for making procedures more systematic (as in a number of OECD Member countries) are being finalised. The main feature of the new system will be the selection of applicants by central entrance examination and employment of those selected according to their qualifications, specialisations and eligibilities.

Training activities for public servants (particularly for those employed at reception desks and having direct contacts with the public) have been conducted since the beginning of 1990, in order to improve relations between the citizen and the administration with a view to improving responsiveness. These training activities will be repeated annually under the auspices of the Prime Minister's Office.

Introduction and Use of Information Technology

Parallel to the widespread use of information technology in public administration, a more systematic method of coding and filing has been developed with respect to topics and division (unit) codes for the flow of documents between public agencies.

UNITED KINGDOM

Market-type Mechanisms

The privatisation policy continued with the privatisation of the electricity industry (excluding the nuclear industry).

Redistribution of Decision-making Responsibility

By the end of October 1990, 34 Agencies had been established employing nearly 80 000 staff. A further 29 potentially suitable candidates employing nearly 202 000 staff have now been named. These include the Social Security Benefits Agency coming into operation in April 1991, the Passport Office, a number of Defence Support Agencies, Customs and Excise, and the Inland Revenue, which are planning to work fully along "Next Steps" lines. It is expected that by the end of 1991, half the Civil Service will be working in Agencies.

Management improvements are being delivered. This is illustrated in the first annual review of "Next Steps", published at the end of October 1990. The review gives details of all the current Agencies including their business, targets and achievements to date. It also lists all the activities under consideration for Agency status. Significant new developments on the "Next Steps" initiative are expected to be announced in April 1991.

UNITED STATES

During 1990, several key initiatives affecting the authorities of central management agencies were enacted into law. These reforms will have a significant influence on the federal government's own financial management and pay policies, as well as on its budget enforcement and credit reform powers. With the statutory framework in place, much of the emphasis will now shift to implementing the reforms through regulations and other guidance.

Management of Human Resources

The President signed into law in November 1990 a *comprehensive federal pay reform measure* making major changes to the "General Schedule" pay system which covers more than 1.4 million federal civilian employees. The new law will begin a process of linking federal salaries to those paid to comparable workers in local labour markets. This approach contrasts with the existing system, where employees of equal rank receive the same base salary and the same annual pay adjustment, irrespective of where they work. The law sets up a framework for eliminating current pay disparities between the federal and private sectors over the next 12 years.

Prior to providing widespread locality pay adjustments in 1994, the law provides for interim geographic adjustments, up to an additional 8 per cent of base salary in certain high-cost areas. The reform would also give federal managers new flexibilities to provide recruitment, retention, and relocation bonuses to employees, as well as increased awards for superior performance. The statute creates a separate new pay system for law enforcement officers emphasising a regional pay-setting approach, as well as new authorities to hire up to 800 "critical positions" to be paid special, higher salaries up to the rate of cabinet officers ($138 900 as of January 1991). The statute also sets up a senior biomedical corps to include up to 350 outstanding individuals in the field of biomedical or clinical research whose pay likewise may be set at or below that of a cabinet officer.

In a related compensation development, the salaries of most top U.S. Government officials will increase by 29 per cent in January 1991. The pay raises will cover judges, members of the House of Representatives, and the highest ranking executive branch officials. The pay increases were authorised by the Ethics Reform Act signed by the President in November 1989. The pay of U.S. Senators will rise by somewhat less than 4 per cent, since the Senate elected to continue receiving honoraria for speeches, appearances, and articles in lieu of the larger salary increases. In addition, the pay for more than 8 000 members of the Senior Executive Service (SES) and Senior Foreign Service (SFS) will increase from 22 to 29 per cent.

Performance, Accountability and Control

New legislation establishing a *formal, integrated structure for financial management activities* in federal agencies was signed by the President in November 1990. The act sets goals and reporting requirements for improved accounting systems, financial management, and internal controls. It also includes new requirements for the preparation and audit of financial statements by executive agencies. The statute creates a Deputy Director for Management within the Office of Management and Budget (OMB) who is the chief official responsible for financial management in the federal government, as well as for procurement, regulatory and general management activities.

The act requires the Presidential appointment of a *Chief Financial Officer* (CFO) in 23 agencies, including all cabinet departments and several large agencies. The CFOs report to the head of each of their respective departments and agencies. The new act stipulates that agencies must prepare annual financial statements covering revolving funds, trust funds, and commercial functions covering fiscal year 1991 and beyond. The OMB is charged with prescribing the form and content of the financial statements.

Under a separate new statute implementing the recent U.S. budget *deficit reduction agreement,* the administration will be using revised ground rules to enforce budget deficit targets. The statute sets discretionary spending caps in three categories for fiscal years 1991-93: domestic, defense, and international. It also establishes a series of "sequester reports" at specified times during the year to anticipate and monitor developments on deficit reduction. Additionally, the statute sets up a special "sequester report" process which would be triggered if a particular appropriation bill causes a breach in planned discretionary spending levels. If that situation occurs, the President is to issue a sequester order which reduces the level of spending in the specific appropriation so that the overall spending targets are preserved.

The new budget deficit reduction law also contains provisions that require more precise costing of direct and guaranteed federal loan programmes. The reforms will place the cost of credit programmes on a budgetary basis that is equivalent to other federal expenditures. Federal credit programmes are currently displayed on a cash accounting basis, which tends to overstate the cost of direct loans and understate guaranteed loan costs. Beginning in fiscal year 1992, however, the government's long-term credit costs will be calculated on a net present value basis. For non-entitlement spending programmes, this new approach will require federal agencies to request annual appropriations or funding limitations to cover the costs of direct loans obligated or loan guarantees committed. Both the OMB and the Congressional Budget Office in the legislative branch will be working closely on guidelines for preparing credit cost estimates and on improved costing methodologies for the future.

Management of Policy-making

During the past several years, the use of formal programme evaluations at the federal level tended to decline. In 1990, however, the pace of programme evaluation activity has started to accelerate. For example, one major evaluation has started in the Department of Health and Human Services focusing on the effectiveness of the "Job Opportunities and Basic Skills" (JOBS) activity — a programme designed to help welfare recipients obtain jobs. In a related evaluation effort, the 1990 Farm Bill authorised large-scale demonstrations of streamlined rules and improved co-ordination between the JOBS programme and the Food Stamp programme's education and training activities. An evaluation will soon be completed on the effectiveness of the Food Stamp programme in aiding registrants to obtain regular employment.

An additional area under evaluation is the vocational rehabilitation programme in the Department of Veterans' Affairs. The evaluation is examining the success rate for veterans' rehabilitation and its cost effectiveness. The assessment will also address the extent to which rehabilitation participants have legitimate employment handicaps.

Market-type Mechanisms: Procurement

The U.S. Congress recently reinvigorated the basic law governing the establishment of the Office of Federal Procurement Policy (OFPP). Under the modification, the OFPP's Administrator has greater authority to manage the federal procurement system to promote, among other things, full and open competition, continued development of a competent, professional workforce, and equitable relationships with the private sector. The strengthened role of the OFPP within the OMB will help ensure that proper procurement policies are developed government-wide to support market-type mechanisms.

Supplementary Reference Material

Public Law 101-576, November 15, 1990, Chief Financial Officers Act of 1990, Washington, D.C.

Public Law 101-509, November 5, 1990, Treasury/Postal Service Appropriation Act (includes the Federal Employees Pay Comparability Act of 1990), Washington, D.C.

Public Law 101-508, November 5, 1990, Budget Reconciliation Act (Title XIII of the Act includes the Budget enforcement and Federal credit reform provisions), Washington, D.C.

Public Law 101-194, November 30, 1989, Ethics Reform Act of 1989 (includes provisions increasing salaries of senior government officials), Washington, D.C.

Annex I

LIST OF NATIONAL CORRESPONDENTS
(as at 1. 1. 91)

Australia
Mr. Malcolm HOLMES
Principal Advisor
General Expenditure Division
Department of Finance
Newlands Street
Parkes, A.C.T. 2600

Austria
Mrs. Lieselotte RICHTER
Oberrat Dkfm. Abteilung IV/7 (Head of Division IV/7)
Bundeskanzleramt (Federal Chancellery)
Ballhausplatz 2
A-1014 *Vienna*

Belgium
M. Jean-Marie MOTTOUL
Chef de Corps des Conseillers de
            la fonction publique
Service d' Administration générale
Cité administrative de l'État
19, boulevard Pachéco, Bte. 2
B-1010 *Bruxelles*

Canada
Mr. Jean-Pierre ROSTAING
Machinery of Government
Privy Council Office
Langevin Block
Ottawa, Ontario K1A 0A3

Denmark
Mr. Tommy JENSEN
Head of Section
Department of Management and Personnel
Ministry of Finance
Bredgade 43-45
DK-1260 *Copenhagen* K

Finland
Mr. Markku KIVINIEMI
Research Manager
Administrative Development Agency
P. L. 101
SF-00331 *Helsinki*

France
Mme Marie-Hélène POINSSOT
Chef de Bureau des méthodes modernes de gestion
Ministère de la fonction publique et des Réformes
administratives
32, rue de Babylone
F-75700 *Paris*

Germany
Dr. Dietmar SEILER
Leitender Regierungsdirektor (Assistant Secretary)
Bundesministerium des Innern
(Federal Ministry of the Interior)
Graurheindorferstrasse, 198
D-5300 *Bonn*

Greece
Dr. Andréas KOKLAS
Senior Officer
Ministry to the Presidency of Government
15, Vassilis Sofias Avenue
GR-106 74 *Athens*

Iceland
Mr. Bolli HÉDINSSON
Economic Adviser to the Prime Minister
Prime Minister's Office
Stjornarradshusid
IS-150 *Reykjavik*

Ireland
Mr. Patrick J. MOORE
Assistant Secretary
Department of Finance
Agriculture House
Kildare Street
Dublin 2

Italy

Mr. Antonino VINCI
Director-General
Department of the Public Service
Presidency of the Council of Ministers
Palazzo Vidoni
Corso Vittorio Emanuele, 116
I-00186 *Rome*

Japan

Mr. Yoshihiro HIGUCHI
Second Secretary
Japanese Delegation to the OECD
7, avenue Hoche
F-75008 *Paris* FRANCE

Luxembourg

M. Pierre NEYENS
Directeur Général
Administration du Personnel de l'État
2, rue Mercier
L-1014 *Luxembourg*

Netherlands

Mr. P.J.M. WILMS
Head of the Office of the Secretary-General
Ministerie van Binnenlandse Zaken
(Ministry of Home Affairs)
Schedeldoekshaven 200
Postbus 20011
NL-2500 EA *The Hague*

New Zealand

Mr. David J. SWALLOW
Deputy State Services Commissioner
Office of the State Services Commission
100 Molesworth Street
P. O. Box 329
Wellington

Norway

Mr. Øystein S. LIEN, Deputy Director General
and Mr. Tom Arne NYGAARD, Senior Executive Officer
Ministry of Labour and Government Administration
Postboks 8004 DEP.
N-0030 *Oslo* 1

Portugal

Mrs. Maria Teresa SANCHES
Director General
Department of Project Evaluation
Ministry of Planning and Regional Development
Praça Duque de Saldanha, 31-4°
P-1000 *Lisbon*

Spain

M. Emilio CASALS PERALTA
Subdirector General de Relaciones Internacionales
Ministerio para las Administraciones Públicas
(Ministry of Public Administration)
Paseo de la Castellana, 3
E-28046 *Madrid*

Sweden

Mr. Lennart ASPEGREN
Under Secretary for Legal and International Affairs
Ministry of Public Administration
S-103 33 *Stockholm*

Switzerland

M. François COUCHEPIN
Vice-Chancelier de la Confédération Suisse
Chancellerie Fédérale
CH-3003 *Berne*

Turkey

Mrs. Reyyan ÖDEMIS
Head
Foreign Affairs Department
Prime Ministry
Bakanliklar
Ankara 06573

United Kingdom

Ms. Pauline DIXON
Senior Executive Officer
OMCS Secretariat
Office of the Minister for the Civil Service
Cabinet Office
Horse Guards Road
London SW1P 3AL

United States

Mr. Steven LIEBERMAN
Assistant Director for General Management
Office of Management and Budget
Executive Office of the President
Washington, D.C. 20503

Yugoslavia

Prof. Eugen PUSIC
Vramceva 1
YU-41000 *Zagreb*

Annex II

STATISTICS

The selection of statistical tables on the government sector which was provided in annex to the publication *Public Management Developments: Survey — 1990* (OECD, Paris, 1990) contained data which had been extracted from OECD publications using a mixture of national and international sources.

In contrast, the tables listed below have been entirely compiled from the OSIRIS database of the OECD using only standardised international sources. This explains why some data are not completely comparable to the figures in the 1990 Survey.

EXPLANATORY NOTE OF MAIN TERMS (OECD definitions)

Labour Force or currently active population: Comprises all persons who fulfill the requirements for inclusion among the employed or unemployed.

Government Sector: Public administration at central, regional and local levels, plus social security funds, excluding public enterprises.

Current Government Disbursements: Current government consumption expenditure, including current transfer payments but excluding capital expenditure.

Main Components of Government Income: Only the three main components have been retained: direct taxes (on income and profits), indirect taxes (on goods and services), and social security contributions. Taken together, they make up about 90 per cent of government income.

Public Debt: The net equals the gross debt of the government sector minus financial assets (essentially government loans for paying social security benefits).

National Investment: Gross fixed capital formation (excluding capital consumption and increases in stocks).

Government Investment: Gross fixed capital formation by the government sector.

.. not available

Table 1a.   SIZE OF THE GOVERNMENT SECTOR, 1989

In terms of employment

	Total population (1 000)	Labour Force, percentage of total population	Total Employment, percentage of labour force	Civilian Employment, percentage of total employment	Government Employment, percentage of total employment
	(1)	(2)	(3)	(4)	(5)
AUSTRALIA	16 833	49.3	93.9	99.1	15.6
AUSTRIA	7 624	45.3	96.9	..	21.1
BELGIUM	9 938	41.7	90.7	97.6	..
CANADA	26 248	51.7	92.5	99.4	20.3
DENMARK	5 132	56.1	91.9	98.7	29.8
FINLAND	4 964	52.0	96.6	98.6	20.6
FRANCE	56 160	43.3	90.6	97.5	22.8
GERMANY	61 990	48.0	93.2	98.1	15.4
GREECE	10 033	39.5	92.5	..	10.4
ICELAND	253	56.1	98.6	..	16.8
IRELAND	3 515	36.8	84.4	98.8	17.9
ITALY	57 525	42.2	88.2	97.4	17.4
JAPAN	123 120	50.9	97.7	..	8.1
LUXEMBOURG	378	48.7	98.9	99.5	..
NETHERLANDS	14 849	45.2	91.7	98.5	15.1
NEW ZEALAND	3 343	47.1	92.9	..	..
NORWAY	4 227	51.0	95.1	98.3	30.8
PORTUGAL	10 337	45.2	95.0	98.5	14.1
SPAIN	38 888	39.0	83.1	97.3	14.3
SWEDEN	8 493	53.3	98.7	..	31.5
SWITZERLAND	6 723	52.6	99.5	..	10.6
TURKEY	55 255	34.7	90.0	97.1	9.1
UNITED KINGDOM	57 236	49.8	93.9	98.8	19.5
UNITED STATES	248 762	50.5	94.8	98.6	15.1
YUGOSLAVIA	..	..	..	..	..

..   not available.

Sources :   (1) to (4): OECD Labour Force Statistics (OSIRIS Database, segment LFSTG), March 1991.

(5): OECD Analytical Database (segment EOY), March 1991.

Table 1b. SIZE OF THE GOVERNMENT SECTOR, 1988-1989

In terms of expenditure

	GDP per Capita (in $US, current prices, current exchange rates)		Current Government Disbursements, percentage of GDP	
	1988	1989	1988	1989
AUSTRALIA	14.937	16.774	34.2	..
AUSTRIA	16.684	16.590	47.0	..
BELGIUM	15.275	15.393	44.1	..
CANADA	18.738	20.783	40.1	39.6
DENMARK	21.299	20.685	58.6	57.4
FINLAND	21.342	23.261	40.0	39.9
FRANCE	17.101	17.061	46.8	46.5
GERMANY	19.557	19.182	43.8	44.6
GREECE	5.286	5.399	34.0	31.8
ICELAND	23.680	20.516	35.4	36.6
IRELAND	9.250	9.644	..	..
ITALY	14.484	15.051	39.6	41.1
JAPAN	23.235	22.895	34.3	0.0
LUXEMBOURG	17.989	18.564	..	..
NETHERLANDS	15.405	15.064	52.4	50.1
NEW ZEALAND	12.756	12.484	..	..
NORWAY	21.251	21.503	55.1	..
PORTUGAL	4.046	4.386	..	..
SPAIN	8.877	9.772	..	..
SWEDEN	21.551	22.303	61.9	..
SWITZERLAND	27.492	26.350	35.0	34.1
TURKEY	1.313	1.431	..	..
UNITED KINGDOM	14.612	14.633	40.2	39.7
UNITED STATES	19.525	20.630	31.6	..
YUGOSLAVIA	..	..	..	..

.. not available.

Sources : OECD Labour Force Statistics and National Accounts (OSIRIS Database, segments LFSTG, INCOUT and GDP-DOLL), March 1991.

Table 2.   TRENDS IN GOVERNMENT SOCIAL EXPENDITURE, 1980-1988

Percentage of final consumption expenditure/GDP*

	Total Final Consumption Expenditure		Education		Health		Social Security and Welfare	
	1980	1988	1980	1988	1980	1988	1980	1988
AUSTRALIA	17.8	16.7	4.5	3.8	3.1	3.1	0.5	0.7
AUSTRIA	18.0	18.5	3.9	..	4.4	..	3.3	..
BELGIUM	18.3	15.8	7.0	5.9	..	..	1.3	1.2
CANADA	..	..	..	..	..	..	..	..
DENMARK	..	..	..	..	..	..	..	..
FINLAND	18.1	20.1	4.9	5.1	3.9	4.4	2.3	3.2
FRANCE	..	..	..	..	..	..	..	..
GERMANY	20.1	19.6	4.1	3.7	5.9	6.1	1.9	2.1
GREECE	16.4	20.2	2.2	2.9	1.7	2.3	0.2	0.3
ICELAND	16.4	18.6	3.6	3.9	5.4	7.0	0.8	1.2
IRELAND	..	..	..	..	..	..	..	..
ITALY	14.7	17.0	4.2	4.8	3.0	3.3	0.6	0.7
JAPAN	10.0	9.5	3.7	3.8	0.4	0.4	0.5	0.6
LUXEMBOURG	..	..	..	..	..	..	..	..
NETHERLANDS	17.9	15.8	6.3	4.9	..	..	0.7	0.8
NEW ZEALAND	..	..	..	..	..	..	..	..
NORWAY	18.8	21.0	5.1	5.4	4.1	4.9	1.6	2.1
PORTUGAL	14.5	..	3.4	..	2.6	..	0.9	..
SPAIN	..	..	..	..	..	..	..	..
SWEDEN	29.1	26.0	5.9	..	7.3	..	4.8	..
SWITZERLAND	..	..	..	..	..	..	..	..
TURKEY	..	..	..	..	..	..	..	..
UNITED KINGDOM	21.2	19.6	4.3	3.8	4.7	4.6	1.4	1.4
UNITED STATES	17.6	18.4	4.6	4.5	1.0	0.9	0.6	0.6
YUGOSLAVIA	..	..	..	..	..	..	..	..

.. not available.

Source :   OECD National Accounts (OSIRIS Database, segments GDP and GOVE), March 1991.
     * The 1990 table covered total outlays.

Table 3. TRENDS IN GOVERNMENT TAX INCOME, 1980-1988

Percentage of GDP

	Total Taxes		On Income and Profits		Social Security Contributions		On goods and and services	
	1980	1988	1980	1988	1980	1988	1980	1988
AUSTRALIA	28.6	30.8	16.0	17.4	..	..	8.9	8.6
AUSTRIA	41.2	41.9	11.0	10.8	12.7	13.7	13.0	13.4
BELGIUM	43.5	45.1	17.8	17.5	13.2	15.2	11.4	11.2
CANADA	31.6	34.0	14.7	15.7	3.3	4.5	10.3	10.2
DENMARK	45.5	52.1	25.0	30.5	0.8	1.2	17.0	17.8
FINLAND	33.0	37.9	16.2	19.1	3.1	3.1	12.8	14.3
FRANCE	41.7	44.4	7.6	7.7	17.8	19.2	12.7	13.1
GERMANY	38.0	37.4	13.3	12.8	13.1	14.0	10.3	9.4
GREECE	29.4	35.9	5.7	6.4	9.7	11.7	12.1	16.3
ICELAND	30.5	31.7	7.8	8.4	0.7	0.8	18.3	18.1
IRELAND	34.0	41.5	12.4	16.0	4.9	5.8	14.9	17.4
ITALY	30.2	37.1	9.4	13.2	11.5	12.4	8.0	10.4
JAPAN	25.5	31.3	11.7	14.8	7.4	9.1	4.2	3.9
LUXEMBOURG	40.9	42.8	17.7	17.8	12.0	10.9	8.6	10.8
NETHERLANDS	45.8	48.2	15.1	13.4	17.4	20.4	11.6	12.5
NEW ZEALAND	33.1	37.9	23.1	22.7	..	..	7.4	12.0
NORWAY	47.1	46.9	19.4	15.7	9.9	12.0	16.7	17.6
PORTUGAL	28.7	34.6	5.7	7.7	8.5	9.3	12.9	16.6
SPAIN	24.1	32.8	6.3	9.7	11.7	11.7	5.0	10.0
SWEDEN	49.1	55.3	21.3	24.3	14.1	13.9	11.8	13.4
SWITZERLAND	30.8	32.5	12.7	13.2	9.5	10.4	6.3	6.1
TURKEY	21.7	22.9	11.2	7.8	3.0	3.4	5.6	7.3
UNITED KINGDOM	35.4	37.3	13.5	14.0	5.9	6.9	10.3	11.6
UNITED STATES	29.5	29.8	13.9	12.8	7.7	8.8	4.9	5.0
YUGOSLAVIA	..	..	..	..	..	..	..	0.0

.. not available.

Source : OECD Revenue Statistics (OSIRIS Database, segment TAXREV), March 1991.

Table 4.   TRENDS IN GOVERNMENT EMPLOYMENT, 1980-1990

Percentage of total employment

	1980	1985	1988	1989	1990
AUSTRALIA	16.0	17.5	16.5	15.6	15.6
AUSTRIA	17.6	19.4	20.9	21.1	20.8
BELGIUM	18.7	20.2	..	..	..
CANADA	19.4	20.8	20.3	20.3	20.6
DENMARK	28.3	29.7	29.4	29.8	29.9
FINLAND	17.2	19.2	20.6	20.6	20.9
FRANCE	20.0	22.7	22.9	22.8	22.6
GERMANY	14.6	15.6	15.5	15.4	15.2
GREECE	8.9	9.9	10.1	10.4	10.2
ICELAND	15.7	16.5	16.9	16.8	17.3
IRELAND	16.4	18.8	18.4	17.9	17.2
ITALY	15.7	16.8	17.3	17.4	17.2
JAPAN	8.8	8.7	8.3	8.1	7.9
LUXEMBOURG	..	..	..	..	..
NETHERLANDS	14.8	16.0	15.4	15.1	14.9
NEW ZEALAND	17.2	14.9	..	..	
NORWAY	25.3	29.2	29.3	30.8	32.0
PORTUGAL	10.7	13.2	14.1	14.1	14.3
SPAIN	10.5	13.4	14.1	14.3	14.5
SWEDEN	30.7	32.9	31.8	31.5	31.8
SWITZERLAND	10.1	10.3	10.5	10.6	10.6
TURKEY	10.5	9.1	9.1	9.1	9.3
UNITED KINGDOM	21.3	21.7	20.7	19.5	19.1
UNITED STATES	16.4	15.3	15.1	15.1	15.5
YUGOSLAVIA	..	..	..	..	..

..   not available.

Source :   OECD Analytical Database (segment EOY), March 1991.

Table 5.   TRENDS IN GOVERNMENT CURRENT DISBURSEMENTS, 1976–1989

Percentage of GDP

	1976	1980	1985	1986	1987	1988	1989
AUSTRALIA	29.8	30.7	34.1	35.2	35.0	34.2	..
AUSTRIA	42.4	46.4	48.5	48.2	47.9	47.0	..
BELGIUM	40.1	42.7	45.9	45.1	45.4	44.1	..
CANADA	35.8	36.2	38.7	39.5	40.0	40.1	39.6
DENMARK	46.9	52.2	56.5	58.3	58.8	58.6	57.4
FINLAND	41.0	35.8	40.5	41.8	39.7	40.0	39.9
FRANCE	41.8	44.5	47.6	46.9	47.4	46.8	46.5
GERMANY	44.0	44.7	45.6	44.9	44.4	43.8	44.6
GREECE	29.5	30.5	34.6	35.6	36.5	34.0	31.8
ICELAND	33.0	33.3	32.5	32.1	32.1	35.4	36.6
IRELAND	37.9	38.8	43.6	43.5	43.7	..	..
ITALY	..	33.0	38.0	39.0	39.2	39.6	41.1
JAPAN	23.6	27.6	31.2	31.5	33.4	34.3	0.0
LUXEMBOURG	50.2	53.3	55.9	52.9	..	..	..
NETHERLANDS	49.5	52.8	54.3	53.0	53.6	52.4	50.1
NEW ZEALAND	..	..	..	..	..	..	..
NORWAY	49.8	53.2	55.1	54.7	55.2	55.1	..
PORTUGAL	..	31.4	35.9	37.6	..	..	..
SPAIN	..	29.7	34.5	35.0	..	..	..
SWEDEN	..	56.3	59.5	60.4	62.2	61.9	..
SWITZERLAND	33.9	32.8	34.4	35.0	34.5	35.0	34.1
TURKEY	..	..	..	..	..	..	..
UNITED KINGDOM	39.7	39.9	42.2	41.2	40.6	40.2	39.7
UNITED STATES	29.5	30.8	31.3	31.4	..	31.6	..
YUGOSLAVIA	..	..	..	..	..	..	..

.. not available.

Source : OECD National Accounts (OSIRIS Database, segments GDP and INCOUT), March 1991.

Table 6.   TRENDS IN NET AND GROSS PUBLIC DEBT, 1980-1990

Percentage of GNP/GDP

	NET					GROSS				
	1980	1985	1988	1989	1990	1980	1985	1988	1989	1990
AUSTRALIA	24.9	26.3	18.7	14.0	10.2	24.9	26.4	18.7	14.9	11.1
AUSTRIA	37.2	49.6	59.0	57.9	55.7	37.2	49.6	57.4	56.4	53.7
BELGIUM	..	..	..	..	..	79.9	122.7	134.5	..	..
CANADA	12.9	32.8	37.2	37.8	40.3	45.1	64.6	69.0	68.7	71.0
DENMARK	7.3	34.4	26.6	25.8	25.9	33.5	64.1	54.4	54.0	53.7
FINLAND	−6.1	0.9	0.6	−2.3	−4.5	13.9	19.0	..	17.0	15.4
FRANCE	14.3	22.9	25.2	24.8	24.4	37.3	45.4	46.9	46.3	46.0
GERMANY	14.3	21.9	23.5	22.1	22.0	32.5	42.2	44.4	43.1	41.5
GREECE	27.8	57.9	71.0	78.5	82.4	27.7	57.9	71.8	75.6	79.8
ICELAND	..	..	..	..	..	..	..	..	..	..
IRELAND	78.0	122.0	134.2	124.8	117.1	78.0	122.1	131.9	122.6	114.5
ITALY	54.0	81.3	93.7	95.6	97.2	59.0	84.0	..	96.8	98.4
JAPAN	17.3	26.3	17.7	13.9	9.8	52.0	68.2	..	68.4	65.1
LUXEMBOURG	..	..	..	..	..	..	..	..	..	..
NETHERLANDS	24.9	43.0	55.1	58.0	60.0	45.9	69.6	78.0	79.8	80.4
NEW ZEALAND	..	..	..	..	..	..	..	..	..	..
NORWAY	0.4	−16.0	−26.0	−25.4	−25.5	52.2	40.7	41.8	43.1	42.4
PORTUGAL	..	..	..	..	..	..	..	62.3	59.6	55.3
SPAIN	7.9	27.9	31.2	30.3	30.5	18.7	47.2	48.1	47.0	46.0
SWEDEN	−13.5	16.1	2.1	−3.4	−7.5	44.5	67.7	58.2	54.0	49.4
SWITZERLAND	..	..	..	..	..	..	..	17.7	12.0	6.9
TURKEY	..	..	..	..	..	..	..	..	..	..
UNITED KINGDOM	47.3	46.3	37.2	33.2	30.7	54.1	53.1	..	40.0	36.2
UNITED STATES	18.6	27.4	31.4	30.7	30.4	37.7	48.8	..	51.5	52.0
YUGOSLAVIA	..	..	..	..	..	..	..	..	..	..

.. not available.

Source : OECD Analytical Database (segment EOY), March 1991.

Table 7.   TRENDS IN GOVERNMENT INVESTMENT, 1974-1989

Percentage of GNP and of National Investment (NI)

	GNP	NI	GNP	NI	GNP	NI	GNP	NI	GNP	NI
	1974		1980		1987		1988		1989	
AUSTRALIA	4.0	17.0	2.9	11.9	2.8	11.7	2.3	9.3	2.3	9.0
AUSTRIA	5.1	17.9	4.2	16.3	3.4	14.8	3.2	13.6	3.2	13.3
BELGIUM	3.4	15.1	3.6	17.3	1.8	11.3	..	..	..	..
CANADA	3.6	15.1	2.7	11.4	2.3	11.1	2.3	10.4	2.3	10.7
DENMARK	3.8	15.8	3.4	18.2	2.2	11.8	2.4	13.5	2.3	13.0
FINLAND	3.2	10.8	3.2	12.4	3.3	13.9	3.1	12.3	2.9	10.5
FRANCE	3.4	13.2	3.1	13.4	3.0	15.4	3.1	15.3	3.2	15.3
GERMANY	4.1	18.8	3.6	15.8	2.4	12.3	2.3	11.7	2.3	11.5
GREECE	3.4	15.1	2.5	10.5	3.2	19.3	3.1	18.2	3.1	17.0
ICELAND	..	..	9.0	35.5	5.0	25.3	5.0	26.7	5.1	28.8
IRELAND	6.0	23.9	6.1	20.3	3.2	17.3	2.3	12.1	1.7	8.4
ITALY	3.0	11.7	3.2	13.1	3.5	17.9	3.5	17.5	3.5	17.7
JAPAN	5.2	15.0	6.1	19.4	5.0	17.7	5.1	17.0	4.9	16.0
LUXEMBOURG	4.7	19.0	6.3	23.3	5.2	20.7	..	..	..	..
NETHERLANDS	3.7	16.7	3.3	15.5	2.4	11.8	2.4	10.9	2.3	10.6
NEW ZEALAND	7.7	29.5	6.3	30.2	4.7	21.5	..	..	..	..
NORWAY	4.6	15.2	4.0	16.2	3.6	12.8	3.9	13.4	3.7	13.6
PORTUGAL	2.3	8.9	4.1	14.5	2.7	11.0	2.9	11.0	2.8	10.3
SPAIN	2.4	8.6	1.8	8.2	3.3	16.1	3.8	16.9	4.3	18.0
SWEDEN	3.6	16.2	3.3	17.0	2.3	12.2	2.4	12.2	2.4	11.4
SWITZERLAND	5.0	18.2	3.8	15.9	3.1	12.2	3.1	11.7	3.0	11.3
TURKEY	8.2	45.0	10.9	56.1	12.8	53.4	9.9	41.0	9.6	42.8
UNITED KINGDOM	5.2	25.1	2.4	13.2	1.7	9.7	1.3	6.8	1.8	8.9
UNITED STATES	..	..	..	..	..	..	..	..	..	..
YUGOSLAVIA	..	..	..	..	..	..	..	..	..	..

..   not available.

Source :   OECD Analytical Database (segment EOY), March 1991.

WHERE TO OBTAIN OECD PUBLICATIONS – OÙ OBTENIR LES PUBLICATIONS DE L'OCDE

Argentina – Argentine
CARLOS HIRSCH S.R.L.
Galería Güemes, Florida 165, 4° Piso
1333 Buenos Aires   Tel. 30.7122, 331.1787 y 331.2391
Telegram: Hirsch-Baires
Telex: 21112 UAPE-AR. Ref. s/2901
Telefax:(1)331-1787

Australia – Australie
D.A. Book (Aust.) Pty. Ltd.
648 Whitehorse Road, P.O.B 163
Mitcham, Victoria 3132   Tel. (03)873.4411
Telefax: (03)873.5679

Austria – Autriche
OECD Publications and Information Centre
Schedestrasse 7
D-W 5300 Bonn 1 (Germany)   Tel. (49.228)21.60.45
Telefax: (49.228)26.11.04
Gerold & Co.
Graben 31
Wien I   Tel. (0222)533.50.14

Belgium – Belgique
Jean De Lannoy
Avenue du Roi 202
B-1060 Bruxelles   Tel. (02)538.51.69/538.08.41
Telex: 63220   Telefax: (02) 538.08.41

Canada
Renouf Publishing Company Ltd.
1294 Algoma Road
Ottawa, ON K1B 3W8   Tel. (613)741.4333
Telex: 053-4783   Telefax: (613)741.5439
Stores:
61 Sparks Street
Ottawa, ON K1P 5R1   Tel. (613)238.8985
211 Yonge Street
Toronto, ON M5B 1M4   Tel. (416)363.3171
Federal Publications
165 University Avenue
Toronto, ON M5H 3B8   Tel. (416)581.1552
Telefax: (416)581.1743
Les Publications Fédérales
1185 rue de l'Université
Montréal, PQ H3B 3A7   Tel.(514)954-1633
Les Éditions La Liberté Inc.
3020 Chemin Sainte-Foy
Sainte-Foy, PQ G1X 3V6   Tel. (418)658.3763
Telefax: (418)658.3763

Denmark – Danemark
Munksgaard Export and Subscription Service
35, Nørre Søgade, P.O. Box 2148
DK-1016 København K   Tel. (45 33)12.85.70
Telex: 19431 MUNKS DK   Telefax: (45 33)12.93.87

Finland – Finlande
Akateeminen Kirjakauppa
Keskuskatu 1, P.O. Box 128
00100 Helsinki   Tel. (358 0)12141
Telex: 125080   Telefax: (358 0)121.4441

France
OECD/OCDE
Mail Orders/Commandes par correspondance:
2, rue André-Pascal
75775 Paris Cédex 16   Tel. (33-1)45.24.82.00
Bookshop/Librairie:
33, rue Octave-Feuillet
75016 Paris   Tel. (33-1)45.24.81.67
(33-1)45.24.81.81
Telex: 620 160 OCDE
Telefax: (33-1)45.24.85.00 (33-1)45.24.81.76
Librairie de l'Université
12a, rue Nazareth
13100 Aix-en-Provence   Tel. 42.26.18.08
Telefax : 42.26.63.26

Germany – Allemagne
OECD Publications and Information Centre
Schedestrasse 7
D-W 5300 Bonn 1   Tel. (0228)21.60.45
Telefax: (0228)26.11.04

Greece – Grèce
Librairie Kauffmann
28 rue du Stade
105 64 Athens   Tel. 322.21.60
Telex: 218187 LIKA Gr

Hong Kong
Swindon Book Co. Ltd.
13 - 15 Lock Road
Kowloon, Hong Kong   Tel. 366.80.31
Telex: 50 441 SWIN HX   Telefax: 739.49.75

Iceland – Islande
Mál Mog Menning
Laugavegi 18, Pósthólf 392
121 Reykjavik   Tel. 15199/24240

India – Inde
Oxford Book and Stationery Co.
Scindia House
New Delhi 110001   Tel. 331.5896/5308
Telex: 31 61990 AM IN
Telefax: (11)332.5993
17 Park Street
Calcutta 700016   Tel. 240832

Indonesia – Indonésie
Pdii-Lipi
P.O. Box 269/JKSMG/88
Jakarta 12790   Tel. 583467
Telex: 62 875

Ireland – Irlande
TDC Publishers – Library Suppliers
12 North Frederick Street
Dublin 1   Tel. 744835/749677
Telex: 33530 TDCP EI   Telefax: 748416

Italy – Italie
Libreria Commissionaria Sansoni
Via Benedetto Fortini, 120/10
Casella Post. 552
50125 Firenze   Tel. (055)64.54.15
Telex: 570466   Telefax: (055)64.12.57
Via Bartolini 29
20155 Milano   Tel. 36.50.83
La diffusione delle pubblicazioni OCSE viene assicurata
dalle principali librerie ed anche da:
Editrice e Libreria Herder
Piazza Montecitorio 120
00186 Roma   Tel. 679.46.28
Telex: NATEL I 621427
Libreria Hoepli
Via Hoepli 5
20121 Milano   Tel. 86.54.46
Telex: 31.33.95   Telefax: (02)805.28.86
Libreria Scientifica
Dott. Lucio de Biasio 'Aeiou'
Via Meravigli 16
20123 Milano   Tel. 805.68.98
Telefax: 800175

Japan – Japon
OECD Publications and Information Centre
Landic Akasaka Building
2-3-4 Akasaka, Minato-ku
Tokyo 107   Tel. (81.3)3586.2016
Telefax: (81.3)3584.7929

Korea – Corée
Kyobo Book Centre Co. Ltd.
P.O. Box 1658, Kwang Hwa Moon
Seoul   Tel. (REP)730.78.91
Telefax: 735.0030

Malaysia/Singapore – Malaisie/Singapour
Co-operative Bookshop Ltd.
University of Malaya
P.O. Box 1127, Jalan Pantai Baru
59700 Kuala Lumpur
Malaysia   Tel. 756.5000/756.5425
Telefax: 757.3661
Information Publications Pte. Ltd.
Pei-Fu Industrial Building
24 New Industrial Road No. 02-06
Singapore 1953   Tel. 283.1786/283.1798
Telefax: 284.8875

Netherlands – Pays-Bas
SDU Uitgeverij
Christoffel Plantijnstraat 2
Postbus 20014
2500 EA's-Gravenhage   Tel. (070 3)78.99.11
Voor bestellingen: Tel. (070 3)78.98.80
Telex: 32486 stdru   Telefax: (070 3)47.63.51

New Zealand – Nouvelle-Zélande
GP Publications Ltd.
Customer Services
33 The Esplanade - P.O. Box 38-900
Petone, Wellington
Tel. (04)685-555   Telefax: (04)685-333

Norway – Norvège
Narvesen Info Center - NIC
Bertrand Narvesens vei 2
P.O. Box 6125 Etterstad
0602 Oslo 6   Tel. (02)57.33.00
Telex: 79668 NIC N   Telefax: (02)68.19.01

Pakistan
Mirza Book Agency
65 Shahrah Quaid-E-Azam
Lahore 3   Tel. 66839
Telex: 44886 UBL PK. Attn: MIRZA BK

Portugal
Livraria Portugal
Rua do Carmo 70-74, Apart. 2681
1117 Lisboa Codex   Tel.: 347.49.82/3/4/5
Telefax: (01) 347.02.64

Singapore/Malaysia – Singapour/Malaisie
See Malaysia/Singapore" – Voir «Malaisie/Singapour»

Spain – Espagne
Mundi-Prensa Libros S.A.
Castelló 37, Apartado 1223
Madrid 28001   Tel. (91) 431.33.99
Telex: 49370 MPLI   Telefax: 575.39.98
Libreria Internacional AEDOS
Consejo de Ciento 391
08009 - Barcelona   Tel. (93) 301-86-15
Telefax: (93) 317-01-41
Llibreria de la Generalitat
Palau Moja, Rambla dels Estudis, 118
08002 - Barcelona   Telefax: (93) 412.18.54
Tel. (93) 318.80.12 (Subscripcions)
(93) 302.67.23 (Publicacions)

Sri Lanka
Centre for Policy Research
c/o Mercantile Credit Ltd.
55, Janadhipathi Mawatha
Colombo 1   Tel. 438471-9, 440346
Telex: 21138 VAVALEX CE   Telefax: 94.1.448900

Sweden – Suède
Fritzes Fackboksföretaget
Box 16356, Regeringsgatan 12
103 27 Stockholm   Tel. (08)23.89.00
Telex: 12387   Telefax: (08)20.50.21
Subscription Agency/Abonnements:
Wennergren-Williams AB
Nordenflychtsvägen 74, Box 30004
104 25 Stockholm   Tel. (08)13.67.00
Telex: 19937   Telefax: (08)618.62.32

Switzerland – Suisse
OECD Publications and Information Centre
Schedestrasse 7
D-W 5300 Bonn 1 (Germany)   Tel. (49.228)21.60.45
Telefax: (49.228)26.11.04
Librairie Payot
6 rue Grenus
1211 Genève 11   Tel. (022)731.89.50
Telex: 28356
Subscription Agency – Service des Abonnements
Naville S.A.
7, rue Lévrier
1201 Genève   Tél.: (022) 732.24.00
Telefax: (022) 738.48.03
Maditec S.A.
Chemin des Palettes 4
1020 Renens/Lausanne   Tel. (021)635.08.65
Telefax: (021)635.07.80
United Nations Bookshop/Librairie des Nations-Unies
Palais des Nations
1211 Genève 10   Tel. (022)734.14.73
Telex: 412962   Telefax: (022)740.09.31

Taiwan – Formose
Good Faith Worldwide Int'l. Co. Ltd.
9th Floor, No. 118, Sec. 2
Chung Hsiao E. Road
Taipei   Tel. 391.7396/391.7397
Telefax: (02) 394.9176

Thailand – Thaïlande
Suksit Siam Co. Ltd.
1715 Rama IV Road, Samyan
Bangkok 5   Tel. 251.1630

Turkey – Turquie
Kültur Yayinlari Is-Türk Ltd. Sti.
Atatürk Bulvari No. 191/Kat. 21
Kavaklidere/Ankara   Tel. 25.07.60
Dolmabahce Cad. No. 29
Besiktas/Istanbul   Tel. 160.71.88
Telex: 43482B

United Kingdom – Royaume-Uni
HMSO
Gen. enquiries   Tel. (071) 873 0011
Postal orders only:
P.O. Box 276, London SW8 5DT
Personal Callers HMSO Bookshop
49 High Holborn, London WC1V 6HB
Telex: 297138   Telefax: 071 873 2000
Branches at: Belfast, Birmingham, Bristol, Edinburgh,
Manchester

United States – États-Unis
OECD Publications and Information Centre
2001 L Street N.W., Suite 700
Washington, D.C. 20036-4910   Tel. (202)785.6323
Telefax: (202)785.0350

Venezuela
Libreria del Este
Avda F. Miranda 52, Aptdo. 60337, Edificio Galipán
Caracas 106   Tel. 951.1705/951.2307/951.1297
Telegram: Libreste Caracas

Yugoslavia – Yougoslavie
Jugoslovenska Knjiga
Knez Mihajlova 2, P.O. Box 36
Beograd   Tel.: (011)621.992
Telex: 12466 jk bgd   Telefax: (011)625.970

Orders and inquiries from countries where Distributors
have not yet been appointed should be sent to: OECD
Publications Service, 2 rue André-Pascal, 75775 Paris
Cedex 16, France.

Les commandes provenant de pays où l'OCDE n'a pas
encore désigné de distributeur devraient être adressées à :
OCDE, Service des Publications, 2, rue André-Pascal,
75775 Paris Cédex 16, France.

75880–7/91

OECD PUBLICATIONS, 2 rue André-Pascal, 75775 PARIS CEDEX 16
PRINTED IN FRANCE
(42 91 01 1) ISBN 92-64-13546-4 - No. 45663 1991